Social Auditing

David H. Blake
William C. Frederick
Mildred S. Myers
with the assistance of
Rogene A. Bucholz
Donald E. Wygal

The Praeger Special Studies program—utilizing the most modern and efficient book production techniques and a selective worldwide distribution network—makes available to the academic, government, and business communities significant, timely research in U.S. and international economic, social, and political development.

Social Auditing
Evaluating the Impact of Corporate Programs

Praeger Publishers   New York   Washington   London

PRAEGER SPECIAL STUDIES IN U.S. ECONOMIC, SOCIAL, AND POLITICAL ISSUES

Library of Congress Cataloging in Publication Data

Blake, David H
    Social auditing.

    (Praeger special studies in U.S. economic, social, and political issues)
    Bibliography: p.
    Includes index.
    1. Industry—Social aspects—United States. 2. Industry—Social aspects—United States—Case studies. I. Frederick, William Crittenden, 1925-   joint author. II. Myers, Mildred S., joint author. III. Title.
HD60.5.U5B55   658.4'08'0973   76-2901
ISBN 0-275-56700-1
ISBN 0-275-85710-7 student ed.

PRAEGER PUBLISHERS
111 Fourth Avenue, New York, N.Y. 10003, U.S.A.

Published in the United States of America in 1976
by Praeger Publishers, Inc.

Printed in the United States of America

This study of social auditing was conducted by the Social Audit Research Group (SARG) of the Graduate School of Business at the University of Pittsburgh from early 1973 through 1974. SARG is composed of three faculty members and several doctoral students of the School.

In conducting the two social audits summarized in the book, SARG had the full cooperation of various officers, managers, and employees of a large business corporation. We gratefully acknowledge their open attitudes and willingness to spend time with members of the audit teams. In the interests of confidentiality and in recognition that the audits were undertaken for the internal use of the company, we are not able to list their names here.

Funds for the study were provided by a series of annual grants from the General Electric Foundation to the School's Research Program on Corporate Social Policy. All views and conclusions contained in the book are those of the authors and should not be attributed to the General Electric Foundation. The members of SARG are grateful to the Foundation for its support and wish to make clear that the audits were not performed in the General Electric Company.

We wish to thank a number of persons who have contributed directly or indirectly to the project: Donald Watson, Ian Wilson, and Joseph Bertotti of the General Electric Company; Arthur Toan of Prince, Waterhouse and Company; Raymond A. Bauer and his research associates in the Harvard Business School; and Jacob Birnberg and Dean H. J. Zoffer of the University of Pittsburgh.

In addition to the principal authors of this book, the members of the Social Audit Research Group included Michael Belch, Rogene Buchholz, Robert Hogner, John Webster, Richard Wokutch, David Wood, and Donald Wygal. Each of these doctoral students made important contributions to the field research, as well as to conceptualizing the unique and sometimes perplexing problems of social auditing. Rogene Buchholz and Donald Wygal deserve special mention as two of the principal auditors and for writing portions of the book.

CONTENTS

1

AN INTRODUCTION TO
SOCIAL AUDITING:
PURPOSE AND PERSPECTIVE

Monitoring a company's social performance—which is what social auditing is all about—is an outgrowth of a great and growing public concern about corporate social responsibility. Larger and larger numbers of people in all walks of life, including many prominent business leaders, now believe that corporations should actively pursue socially responsible goals. That means reducing pollution, building more safety and reliability into products, providing more and better employment and advancement opportunities for minorities and women, making work more meaningful, more satisfying, and safer for all employees, and generally promoting the well-being of society in numerous other ways.

In recent years, social pressure groups representing all of these interests and more have sprung up. Ecologists, blacks, women, consumerists, young people, and white-collar and blue-collar employees have organized significant protest movements aimed at the reform of many corporate practices. Managers of companies have found themselves embroiled in social and political controversies undreamed of in the executive suites of a decade ago. Government at all levels has been brought into these swirling events, enacting new legislation, creating new regulatory agencies, laying down new criteria of performance in several areas of social concern.

The resulting clamor for corporations to display their social concern in tangible ways—by installing costly pollution control equipment, by reducing and eliminating racial and sexual discrimination, by providing greater safeguards and better information for consumers—made almost inevitable the search for systematic ways to monitor a company's social performance. An increasingly wary and skeptical public seemed less and less satisfied with the reassuring messages normally processed through the public relations office. What was wanted—and what would be needed if corporations were to be brought to the bar of public opinion and held accountable for their impact on society—was a way to estimate that social impact.

The traditional economic and financial measures of business performance have been found wanting. Profit stated in dollars is at best only a rough measure of a company's contribution to society. Government regulations and subsidies or private monopolistic arrangements can distort profits, giving false impressions of a firm's economic position and contribution. Even more obvious in recent times is the inability of profits as normally computed to reflect all of the values, attitudes, and expectations of that marvelously complex creature—the consumer.

So the profit yardstick, while useful in many instances as a way of telling business persons what the public thinks of their performance, is obviously being asked to carry too large a burden of accountability. Not only does it fail to measure such elements as racial and sexual discrimination at work, job satisfaction, and employee morale, but also profits are often calculated by formulas that omit social costs to the general community, such as polluted air and dirty waterways.

In an attempt to supplement the usual measures of economic performance, major efforts have been under way since the mid-1960s to construct a system of national social accounts or social indicators. These social indicators are intended to provide ways of estimating the nation's social posture as distinct from the national income accounts, which give some indication of overall economic conditions. In spite of formidable technical, attitudinal, and political difficulties encountered along the way, these efforts to develop a framework of social indicators are well along toward providing a basis for estimating national needs, suggesting priorities, and helping to shape national legislation concerning social matters.

The pressures to develop similar measures of social performance for individual corporations and industries have therefore stemmed from the following four sources: (1) the insistent demands of various social interest groups, (2) the growing acceptance of the belief in corporate social responsibility, (3) the requirements imposed on corporations by governments at all levels to report on specific aspects of social activities such as employment discrimination and environmental pollution, and (4) the general attractiveness of having social reports for individual companies and industries so they may be held accountable to the public for more than just their economic performance, just as the social indicators developed at the national level give a more systematic picture of the nation's overall social well-being than could economic measures alone.

DEFINITION OF SOCIAL AUDITING

The term "social audit" has been applied indiscriminately to a wide range of activities. They include the following practices: (1) an inventory of a company's "social" programs; (2) an inventory of its social "impacts"; (3) cost estimates of various company activities thought to have special social significance; (4) the results of surveys of various company practices regarding environmental pollution, employment discrimination, occupational health and safety, and so on, undertaken at the behest of government regulatory agencies; (5) critical reports or surveys made by persons or organizations external to a company or industry, usually dealing with some particular area of social concern such as sexual discrimination; (6) attempts to determine the attitudes of various groups important to the corporation, such as stockholders, customers, employees, and others; and (7) several other so-called "social audit" efforts.

The term "social audit" itself has been subject to criticism. Some object on the grounds that there are as yet no generally accepted social accounting principles, no professionally recognized independent auditors, and a general lack of agreed-upon criteria against which to measure a corporation's social performance. Such persons, often accountants, perfer the term "social report" or "social information system," signifying that the report and its social information have been drawn along different and less rigorous lines than is true of financial accounting and reporting. Still others believe it to be more realistic to speak of "social accounting," which can probably be made systematic over the long run, while "social auditing"—that is, the independent attesting function—may work out to be a combination of governmental surveillance in mandated areas of social concern and public opinion expressed in tangible but not very systematic ways.

Social auditing is defined here as a systematic attempt to identify, analyze, measure (if possible), evaluate, and monitor the effect of an organization's operations on society (that is, specific social groups) and on the public well-being.

Each of the elements of this definition requires further clarification:

1. "A systematic attempt...": Social auditing requires an orderly, carefully planned series of studies, usually carried out over a rather lengthy time period and ideally repeated in a manner that allows the build-up of a social data base that can be useful for historical comparisons within the organization as well as possibly for comparative purposes between companies.

2. "...to identify...": Identification, often by means of an inventory of an organization's social activities, is a first but continuing step in social auditing. The range of social influences, impacts, and activities can be and usually is quite extensive. Tracking down these various social ramifications has the practical usefulness for management of defining the dimensions and illustrating the complexities of social involvement.

3. "...analyze...": Analysis of the accumulated social data base to determine more precisely its meaning for the company follows naturally from the identification process. A variety of analytical procedures may be employed, ranging from conventional statistical analysis through the use of simple or highly sophisticated attitude-assessment surveys, cost/benefit ratio studies, or the use of informed judgments by experienced social scientists.

4. "...measure (if possible)...": The measurement of social factors for purposes of social auditing or social accounting is relatively underdeveloped when compared with the measurement of economic and financial phenomena. However, the measurement of public opinion, or the attitudes of various populations toward various institutions or issues, or obtaining certain surrogates indicative of such elusive elements as employee morale, or compiling a quantitative record of the hiring, training, promotion, and wage levels of minorities and women, or accumulating quantitative records of various types of environmental pollution—all of these measures are possible and regularly used by both business and government agencies. Measuring the social effects, the social benefits, and the total or "true" social costs of various organizational activities is not presently possible and will probably continue to be an elusive goal of social auditors. Note should be made, though, that the inability of the accounting profession, the business community, and various government offices to achieve complete unanimity of opinion regarding certain critically important economic measures, such as the computation of depreciation charges, has not halted or seriously impaired the usefulness of a variety of financial cost concepts and methods of computation. Social accountants and social auditors, like their counterparts in financial accounting, can work within a range of uncertainty and disagreement over the validity and universality of social cost measurement methods. Some social phenomena can now be measured. It is reasonable to assume that other measurement methods and techniques will be developed as more attention is paid to this area. Social auditors must therefore measure where possible, make informed judgments where necessary, and encourage further research on social measurement in order to develop better tools.

5. "...evaluate...": Evaluation of social performance is the core of social auditing and its ultimate justification. Identification, analysis, and measurement are the preliminary steps taken in order to enable evaluative statements to be made about the social activity under study. The goals of a social program or the norms of performance mandated by government provide examples of an evaluative framework in which informed judgments can be made about the program's effectiveness or the company's performance in achieving specified levels of social activity. The more clearly such goals and norms are stated, the easier is the task of evaluating results. Due to the complexity of many social phenomena and the difficulties of segregating social from economic effects, evaluation may also proceed with more confidence where goals or norms are stated in limited rather than general terms, in narrow rather than broad terms, in precise rather than loose terms, and in operational rather than philosophical terms.

6. "...and monitor...": Monitoring social effects is the follow-up stage of social auditing. It implies a continuing organizational commitment to conduct periodic reviews of the social area in question. For a whole host of reasons— shifting norms or goals, changing technology, new perceptions of social attitudes, newly enacted legislative and administrative rules—previous levels of social

performance may prove to be inadequate. The chances of having to update the social data base are large under these changing circumstances. Continued systematic monitoring of social performance of both the overall organization's efforts as well as that of individual divisions or managers keeps alive and operational the organization's original commitment and protects its investment in any given action that has important social consequences.

7. "...the effect of an organization's operations on society (that is, specific social groups) and on the public well-being." Social effects, impacts, and consequences may flow from the organization's official or declared purposes, as well as from supplementary activities intended to effect some type of social change or to moderate some social condition. Either the social effects are felt directly by some specifically identified social group, such as minority employees or stockholders, whose interests are negatively or positively affected by the organization's activities, or the social consequences of operations may be felt widely by most sectors of society, as in the case of air pollution or unsafe and ineffective products. In the latter cases, "public well-being" in the broadest sense of that term is affected, rather than the perceived well-being of some specific social group.

THE REQUIREMENTS OF SOCIAL AUDITING

Beyond this definition of social auditing, it is important to identify the special requirements that must be present if an organization is to engage in social auditing on a serious basis.

First, the social audit has to conform to specified norms of some kind. These norms may consist of government standards of social performance, goals or standards established by the organization for its activities that create important social impacts, or the perceived or inferred standards of social performance advocated by groups other than the corporation's managers and directors. Unless such norms are present and clearly identified, the social audit cannot reveal whether company performance is effective, ineffective, or neutral, for there will then be no standards against which to measure and evaluate the actual behavior of the organization. For purposes of proceeding with a social audit, the source of such norms is less important than their presence and identification by the auditors. Obviously, participation in the setting of social norms and goals is a matter of critical importance to the organization.

Second, the social audit has to be undertaken with the purpose and intention of influencing company action, programing, or policy in some tangible area of social concern. A genuine social audit is action oriented. It should enable organizational decision makers to act with greater assurance in social areas and on social problems that have previously been either neglected or given lower priority than other kinds of problems. The audit may lead to the initiation or to the termination of various operations that have social consequences for specific groups or for the public in general. The audit may lead to a review of company policies dealing with one or an entire array of operations that are impacting upon society. It may confirm company policies already adopted at an earlier time.

Third, the social audit has to be conducted by professional personnel competent in and knowledgeable about the social area or problem being audited. Most social problems associated with the operations of large-scale organizations prove to be complex and often intractable to simple approaches and solutions. Prolonged study by a variety of experts is sometimes required, if a company is to avoid an uneconomic commitment of resources, poorly timed, directed at the wrong target, and in a quest for unattainable objectives. Where public opinion or the attitudes of specific social groups are an important part of the problem area being audited, it is essential that ways be found to determine those attitudes and to encourage participation of affected groups in productive and creative ways. These things cannot typically be accomplished except by persons who are professionally well informed, socially aware, and capable of employing the appropriate tools of social science for investigating the problem or area of concern.

These three requirements of social auditing rule out a number of activities that are sometimes labeled "social auditing." These latter would include the superficial, hastily conducted, one-time "surveys" of company practices bearing upon one or more social issues; internally generated social reports prepared for public relations purposes only; and the often poorly informed "audits" of various alleged corporate abuses conducted by outsider groups utilizing adverse publicity as a primary tactic. Whatever value these types of activities might have for their practitioners, calling them "social audits" will accomplish little of lasting value, while at the same time tending to conceal the potential practical usefulness and systematic rigorous analysis of a "social audit" as defined above and as used throughout this book.

TYPES OF SOCIAL AUDITS

Several different types of social audits have been either proposed or put into actual practice. Each of these audits conforms to the definition and requirements of social auditing as set forth above. They vary considerably in intent, the group doing the auditing, the methods employed, the form taken by the final audit report, the scope of social action covered, and whether the audit is done by outsiders for critical purposes or by insiders for management review and action.

It will be useful to review each major type of social audit so that their varying characteristics and purposes can be well understood. Such a summary review will also provide the necessary contrast and perspective for understanding the particular type of social audit that is discussed in detail in the present study.

Type I: Social Balance Sheet and Income Statement

Two persons have proposed this type of audit, which envisions the conversion of social costs and benefits into dollar terms and the drawing up of a social statement or social report that would closely parallel some aspects of a conventional financial statement. However, there are important differences in the two proposed approaches.

Clark Abt, the president of Abt Associates, a management consulting firm, has sponsored a social audit of his own firm, as described in the annual reports for 1971, 1972, 1973, and 1974. Careful calculations were made in dollar terms of the social contributions, as well as the social detriments or costs to the community, of the operations of the company. Social assets so stated are balanced against social commitments, obligations, and equity. The result is that "the social balance sheet presents the social net assets to date, expressed as 'Society's Equity' in the social resources of the Company."* On the other hand, "the social income statement represents the net social income provided by company operations to staff, community, general public, and clients. The 'net social income' (social benefits net of costs) is considered to be a social dividend paid out to the staff, community, general public, and clients."

Abt reports further that:

> The basic concept used in the Social Audit to measure social benefits and costs to employees, communities, clients, and the general public is adopted from accounting practice. A thing is assumed to be worth what is paid for it, or what it costs, or the value received from it. This practice assumes all social impacts such as health, security, equality, environment, etc. can be expressed in terms of the money the people concerned have actually paid for the benefits or services, and what they have actually paid to avoid equivalent costs.

In spite of this attempt to emulate the methods and forms of conventional financial accounting, the report notes that "Generally accepted auditing procedures

---

*All quotations are from Abt Associates, Inc., *Annual Report*, Cambridge, Mass., 1971.

have not been developed with respect to such statements, and accordingly our independent auditors are unable to express an opinion thereon."

David Linowes, a certified public accountant with long experience in financial accounting, has proposed that companies draw up a Socio-Economic Operating Statement (SEOS). This report, like the Abt audit, would be stated in dollar terms; it would attempt to balance or compare a firm's social contributions against social costs, and it would be strongly influenced by accounting conventions (the audit team would be headed by a certified public accountant). Unlike the Abt social audit, Linowes would limit the SEOS to only those expenditures undertaken on a voluntary basis. Both social benefits and costs would be reflected by the magnitude of dollars expended, with no allowance for quality variations within the expenditure categories.

Summarized information about this type of social audit is set forth below.

Type I: Social Balance Sheet and Income Statement (Clark Abt and David Linowes)

> *Audit content*: Social performance is stated in dollar terms, using conventional accounting and financial categories
> *Prepared*: Internally by a special team of experts (Abt and Linowes)
> *Auditor*: An external team of experts, headed by a CPA (Linowes)
> *Audience*: Company management and interested public
> *Intended Use*: Management review of cost-benefit ratios; and for report to stockholders
> *Scope*:   Whole Company (Abt)
>   Voluntary activities only (Linowes)
> *Current status*:   Limited use (Abt and Linowes)

Type II: Social Performance Audit

Two organizations have been largely responsible for conducting a type of selective social performance audit. They are the Council on Economic Priorities (CEP), a public-interest research organization, and the Interfaith Center on Corporate Responsibility (ICCR), affiliated with the National Council of Churches and formerly known as the Corporate Information Center. The ICCR conducts research but also assumes an activist-advocacy role eschewed by the CEP.

The social audits undertaken by CEP consist of research-based studies of the performance of selected companies in given industries with respect to some particular area of social or public concern. The viewpoint of the audit is usually negatively critical of company or industry performance. Some areas audited in this way include pollution in the steel industry, the paper pulp industry, and electric-power-generating installations; minority personnel practices of selected banks; and companies active in the production of antipersonnel weapons.

CEP studies are undertaken either with or without the cooperation of the companies being audited. Extensive use is made of data from governmental agencies, particularly where companies refuse to divulge information about company performance.

Since CEP explicitly disclaims being an advocacy organization, the apparent aim of its research studies and published social audits is to expose to public view the actual social performance of companies and industries, with the further assumption that such negative publicity will bring remedial action either by the company and industry itself or by stricter government enforcement of existing laws or the passage of new legislation to curb the highlighted abuses. In its original conception, CEP was intended to provide the financial investment community with systematically developed information about the social performance of companies so that such factors might be taken into consideration in making investment decisions. While that early intention is still present to some extent, a number of CEP's social performance audits provide a scope, a depth of detail, and a negative attitude about industry performance that carry considerably beyond the mere presentation of facts that might be pertinent to investment decisions.

The ICCR combines research and activism. Its major efforts have been directed to highlighting and opposing those companies that operate in or have trade relationships with African nations that suppress majority black populations, particularly the Union of South Africa. It has also studied and publicized the role of selected corporations in the Vietnam-Cambodian wars, the discrimination against women and minorities in corporate personnel practices, and the role of U.S. corporations during the recent military rule of the Philippines.

In addition to publishing detailed reports of company performance in these and other areas of social concern, its representatives often appear at the annual meetings of the targeted corporations to offer a variety of resolutions and proposals for shareholder consideration.

ICCR's social audits are aimed particularly at influencing the investment portfolio decisions made by church organizations affiliated with the National Council of Churches, but their published reports and their activist stance tend to spread their message to wider areas of the interested public.

Summarized information about this type of audit is set forth below.

Type II: Social Performance Audit (Council on Economic Priorities) (Interfaith Center on Corporate Responsibility)

> *Audit content*: A critique of company or industry performance in se-
>   lected areas of social concern—for example, pollution or minority

discrimination or company operations in or with South Africa.
Prepared: Externally by critics
Audience: General investment community and interested public (CEP)
          Church affiliate groups of National Council of Churches
and interested public (ICCR)
Intended Use: Negative publicity for company or industry to influence
investment decisions
Scope   Selected individual companies (ICCR)
          Selected companies representative of an industry (CEP)
Current status: Actively used

Type III: Macro-Micro Social Indicator Audit

This type of social audit would gauge a company's social performance by
how well it achieved consistency during a given period of time with an array or
list of social indicators that signify the public good, the public interest, or the
general well-being of the community in which the company is operating.

Macro social indicators, stated largely in numerical terms, would provide
a framework of goals, criteria, and norms for the general community to achieve
and by which its social state could be calculated. These indicators typically
cover such areas as health and safety, education, housing, transportation, income
levels, cultural activity, citizen participation, and similar items bearing upon
general community well-being. The indicators would be worked out for use at
national, regional, and local community levels.

Micro social indicators, also stated largely in numerical terms, which describe a single company's performance in each of the macro social indicator
areas, would furnish a means for assessing or auditing the company in terms of
its contributions to the well-being of the community. All activities of the company—both those said or intended to be specifically "social" in their impact as
well as those stemming from the concern's main raison d'etre—would be included in these computations.

Two types of comparisons could, in time, be made. One would allow a
company to measure its own social progress in these selected social indicator
areas from year to year. The other comparison would permit one company or
industry to match its social performance against other companies or industries.
In both cases, the general community would have a clearer and more systematically developed picture of company performance in these areas of social concern.

Lee E. Preston and James E. Post of the School of Management at the
State University of New York at Buffalo have proposed such a type of social
performance measurement and reporting.

The First National Bank of Minneapolis has actually carried out such a social audit of its own activities, reporting the results in its annual reports for 1971, 1972, and 1973, and in a separate report for 1974.

A variant of this approach has been proposed but not actually implemented by the Urban Strategy Center of the U.S. Chamber of Commerce.

Summarized information about this type of audit is set forth below.

Type III: Macro-Micro Social Indicator Audit (Preston-Post) (1st National Bank of Minneapolis)

Audit content: Numerical assessment of company performance relative to a set of social indicators developed at national, regional, or local levels

Prepared: Internally by company personnel, at the micro or company level

Externally by public or private agencies, at the macro or community social indicator level

Audience: Company management, shareholders, and interested public

Intended use: Management review of social performance and social impact; communication to shareholders and the public

Scope: Whole company or divisions; or specific programs; in time, intercompany comparisons within industries

Current status: Limited use (1st National Bank of Minneapolis)
Proposed only (Preston-Post)

Type IV: Constituency Group Attitudes Audit

Modern corporations typically interact with a large number of different types of groups, each representing distinctive but sometimes overlapping interests. These groups may include company employees, stockholders, suppliers, customers, the citizenry of local communities, and larger segments of the general public. Corporate actions affect these various groups—sometimes called corporate constituency groups—in diverse ways, and they as well as others are among those that bring social pressures to bear upon the company. Knowing what they think and how they feel about company policies and actions that affect their interests is therefore important for the company's managers.

One type of social audit has been proposed for identifying and measuring the attitudes and preferences of the corporation's constituency groups, so that management would be in a better position to react meaningfully and positively to the diverse social pressures it often feels.

The most comprehensive statement of the corporate constituency attitudes audit has been made by Allan D. Shocker of the University of Pittsburgh and S. Prakash Sethi of the University of California at Berkeley. Adapting marketing methodologies typically used for determining consumer preferences, they propose an analysis that would identify the relevant groups for a given company, specify the criteria of performance important for those groups, construct (and simulate if necessary) social action profiles representing various types of corporate actions affecting the constituency groups, determine the groups' preferences among these various social action possibilities, and analyze these preference judgments to determine what priorities for corporate social action might be inferred from such a process. The proposed methodology is considerably more sophisticated than that employed by other attitude-and-preference surveys, such as the Yankelovich surveys, and would be expected to yield more reliable results. Questionnaires would be used on samples of the various constituency groups.

A similar proposal, not so well worked out, has been suggested by James S. Shulman and Jeffrey Gale of the Massachusetts Institute of Technology. Neither the Shocker-Sethi nor the Shulman-Gale proposals have been tested in practice.

A summary of the major elements of this type of audit is outlined below.

Type IV: Constituency Group Attitudes Audit (Shocker-Sethi) (Shulman-Gale)

> *Audit content*: Analytic measurement of the attitudes and preferences of
>   groups affected by corporate actions regarding various areas and
>   issues of social concern
> *Prepared*: Externally by consultant; eventually perhaps internally by com-
>   pany staff
> *Audience*: Company management (and interested public?)
> *Intended use*: Management review of perceived and desired social impacts
>   and actions (and communication to the public?)
> *Scope*: Whole company or divisions; or specific areas of social concern
> *Current status*: Proposed only

Type V: Government-Mandated Audits

A type of social audit has been employed by various agencies of the federal government—and by their counterparts at state and local levels—in recent years. These agencies include the Environmental Protection Agency (EPA), the Equal Employment Opportunity Commission (EEOC), the Occupational Safety and Health Administration (OSHA), and others.

These audits of company or organizational performance focus upon some particular area of social concern that has been specified in legislation, executive orders, or court decisions as deserving of governmental surveillance, monitoring, and enforcement. These agencies may compel companies or organizations to disclose information regarding various types of environmental pollution (EPA), various forms of employment discrimination (EEOC), and injuries and deaths associated with occupational activities (OSHA). In some cases, they may specify standards of performance, suggest specific programmatic actions and time tables of compliance, and seek court orders to compel compliance. The monitoring of an organization's social performance in these various areas of social concern is, theoretically at least, a continuing function.

Such government-mandated audits typically describe, usually in numerical and statistical terms, prevailing patterns of pollution or discrimination or industrial accidents and casualties. The audit may also discuss the economic, technological, organizational, and attitudinal elements contributing to the problem, as well as those that may be recommended to rectify the situation.

A summary of the major elements of this type of social audit is set forth below.

Type V: Government-Mandated Audits (Environmental Protection Agency) (Equal Employment Opportunity Commission) (Occupational Safety and Health Administration)

> *Audit content*: Analytic or numerical measurement of the organization's performance in the mandated area (environmental pollution, employment discrimination, industrial casualties), plus description of practices, policies, and organizational features that contribute to the problem
>
> *Prepared*: Internally by company personnel, at the request of the auditing agency or as specified by law
>
> *Auditor*: The respective governmental agency
>
> *Intended use*: Advocacy and enforcement of government-defined norms of social performance in the mandated area
>
> *Scope*: Whole company or division
>
> *Current status*: Actively used

Type VI: Social Process/Program Management Audit

The social process audit, sometimes called the program management audit, is an attempt to determine the effectiveness of selected programs of an organization that have social significance or social impact. The auditors analyze the process by which the program came into existence (that is, its history), the process by which the program goals were established (that is, the various social forces at work within and outside the company that led to this particular program and its goals), the process by which program inputs are transformed into program outputs (that is, a socioeconomic input-output analysis), and the process by which the program is, or could conceivably be, evaluated.

This auditing approach accepts as given the goals established for the program by the organization's management. The purpose of the audit is to develop a systematic basis of information about the program that will enable management to review its effectiveness in meeting those goals and to allow management to evaluate the program's appropriateness vis-a-vis alternative uses of those resources.

A type of cost-benefit analysis is attempted, in full recognition that sufficient information is typically lacking that would permit a rigorous quantitative statement of full costs or an analysis of opportunity costs. Direct costs (in money and time) and allocated costs are computed where such data are available in usable form, and these cost figures are developed both for the organization sponsoring the program and for the noncompany persons or organizations affected by the program. Broader social costs, such as public health hazards from pollutants, which are borne by large segments of the population, are also taken into account, where feasible.

The calculation and analysis of benefits are likewise a blend of quantifiable and nonquantifiable elements derived from the program by the company and by the affected noncompany parties. Many of these benefits are not precisely measurable nor can they always be converted into monetary terms. They involve such fugitive elements as employee morale, organizational loyalty, personal values infused into program administration, attitudes of community persons toward the company or toward business in general, and the many informal systems of communication, reward, and punishment that operate among the employees of the organization. Finding out about such factors as these requires the abandonment of a strictly quantitative approach and the adoption of a variety of research techniques and methods developed and used by social scientists. These methods may include participant-observer roles, attitude surveys, in-depth interviews guided by carefully designed interview schedules, and others.

In brief, the social process/program management audit is a description and a quantitative and nonquantitative analysis of a specific program activity, intended to provide management with systematically developed information for purposes of review of program effectiveness in achieving the company's stated goals. This type of audit is for internal use, although management may also choose to disclose its results to others such as stockholders or various segments of the interested public. It deals, not with the entire company and its overall social performance, but only with clearly identifiable and specific programs. It does not attempt to compare program performance in one area with program performance in another area, although in time a sufficient base for doing so might be built up within a given organization.

Two organizations have been active in conducting this type of social audit. One is the Social Audit Research Group (SARG) of the Graduate School of Business at the University of Pittsburgh. In addition, the Bank of America has applied the method to some of its programs.

A summary of the major elements of this type of social audit is set forth below.

Type VI: Social Process/Program Management Audit (Social Audit Research group) (Bank of America)

> *Audit content*: Quantitative, descriptive, and social-science analytic assessment of organizational performance in selected programs having social significance and impact
> *Prepared*: Internally by consultant team (SARG)
> Internally by company personnel (Bank of America)
> *Audience*: Company management (and interested public?)
> *Intended use*: Management review of program effectiveness (and communication with public?)
> *Scope*: Specific programs only
> *Current status*: Actively used (SARG and Bank of America)

THE SOCIAL PROCESS AUDIT

The prime purpose of this book is to describe the procedures involved in conducting a social process audit (Type VI, summarized above). An audit methodology, an implementation plan, and a report format are described in sufficient detail to provide guidance to those wishing to undertake such an audit or who may have organizational responsibility for supervising one. Two case studies illustrating the social process audit as actually carried out in a large industrial corporation are outlined and discussed.

Advantages

The choice of this type of social audit has been made for several important and compelling reasons.

There is, first of all, the problem of minimizing the methodological difficulties and shortcomings that characteristically plague this new field of social measurement and evaluation. These problems, which are discussed in the following chapter, include the lack of widely accepted standards for judging social performance, the difficulty of systematically measuring some types of social phenomena, the occasional absence of social data essential for a comprehensive analysis or its appearance in a form that is inappropriate for the purposes of a social audit, and the sheer magnitude and complexity of the social factors that are typically involved in any attempt to assess a large-scale organization's impact upon the society in which it operates, with attendant high-level expenditures of time, money, and professional expertise.

Some of these vexing technical problems can be avoided or reduced to manageable proportions by adopting the social process audit approach. The size and complexity of the task can be greatly reduced by singling out a specific program or activity and concentrating auditing efforts on that area rather than attempting to assay the entire spectrum of an organization's social influences and impacts. With today's large, diversified, divisionalized, multinational corporations, the latter task becomes an impressively ambitious undertaking, probably beyond the will, the resources, and the technical capabilities of most if not all companies.

However, a beginning can be made by giving close, systematic attention to specific, identifiable programs or activities that have obvious social implications, such as charitable contributions to community organizations, or that are the subject of special regulatory attention by government agencies, such as employment discrimination or environmental pollution. Such programs or activities may have company-wide dimensions or they may be most meaningfully analyzed on a divisional or a local operating-unit basis. In either case, the audited activities typically appear as operational problems to be acted upon at divisional, departmental, or local plant levels and not simply at a headquarters level. The social process audit is a method for systematically analyzing and evaluating such programs and activities in a limited operational context, thereby reducing the social auditing task to manageable proportions and producing a range of data that can be comprehended and dealt with by operating managers. Costs and time expended on the audit are also reduced, as compared with attempts to measure an organization's total social impact.

By focusing upon the goals set by the company for its various social programs and keying the audit to those organizationally determined criteria, the social process auditor avoids, for purposes of any given audit, the very real dilemma, facing the entire field of social auditing, of lack of general consensus on criteria for judging corporate social performance. Whether various social interest groups or government agencies will agree that a particular organization is "measuring up" to their expectations or to mandated performance criteria is one type of problem that will probably be with us indefinitely, although in time one might hope and perhaps expect that further development and refinement of national, regional, and local social indicators will result in a reasonable degree of consensus about desired levels of social performance. In the meantime, any given organization, working within its own framework of goals and objectives, can proceed in systematic fashion to analyze the results of specifically identifiable programs and activities that have obvious social consequences.

The problems of data availability and data morphology are probably more severe at an aggregate societal level than at the organizational level. Social information is often, but not always, embedded in existing company records but has not been collected or classified for purposes of social analysis. Even where such information has not been compiled, that task is less formidable for a single company, division, or operating unit when the data will be used internally for management review of program effectiveness, as contrasted with the collection and reporting of information to be used by external persons or groups for generalized or diverse purposes. Moreover, the audit process itself helps to define data needs by revealing information gaps and by suggesting, again in operational terms, the particular form the data should assume in order to be of maximum usefulness to the organization's managers.

The difficulty and at times the downright impossibility of finding adequate measures for certain types and ranges of human phenomena—for example, "true" or total social costs of a particular action, or the extent and psychological-sociological dimensions of racial and sexual discrimination, or the full effects on human health of various types of environmental pollutants—will be as characteristic of the social process audit as of other approaches to social auditing, since this problem is generic to all social measurement endeavors. But the present inability to find perfect measures for all social phenomena does not mean that limited measures should not be used to achieve as close an approximation as feasible, while the search continues for more adequate ways to estimate and analyze social influences and social impacts.

The foregoing discussion therefore suggests that several of the troublesome methodological problems associated with early attempts to make social auditing a useful tool of social analysis and decision making can be minimized by adopting the social process audit. Additionally, other advantages exist that are of equal or possibly greater importance.

While the entire area of social measurement and social accounting carries an undoubted stigma of generality and vagueness when compared with other measurement efforts such as financial enterprise accounting or national income accounting, a more tangible and definite image of social auditing emerges when specific, identifiable social programs or activities are the target of such measurement efforts. For example, a firm's pollution control activities are visible, measurable, quantifiable, and can be made subject to rigorous analytic treatment. Government pollution control criteria are available, often imposed, and provide a tangible framework against which the organization's performance can be analyzed. Some, though not all, effects on public health are known from specific pollutants. Economic costs of pollution can be estimated within fairly reasonable ranges of probability.

Similarly, other areas of social concern, such as various types of employment discrimination or occupational injuries and hazards or product effectiveness and safety, often appear as well-defined programmatic activities subject to the same kinds of managerial discipline, organization, analysis, and decision making as would be true of economic or financial activities. A social process audit of any one of these discrete areas of organizational concern provides operating managers with tangible, practical information that can be useful, or indeed indispensable, for decision making and policy review. Whereas measuring the company's entire range of social impacts may be so complex and large-scale as to elude the combined skills of social auditors and company management, the existence of clearly identifiable social programs and activities not only reduces and simplifies all technical problems of social auditing but renders social analysis less esoteric to managers who prefer to use "hard" data for their decisions. The target of the social process audit—analysis of identifiable programs and activities with obvious social consequences—is therefore seen to be a reasonable, attainable, and practical activity that has a high likelihood of producing operational information for organizational managers and policy makers.

The problems associated with gaining management acceptance of any type of social auditing are discussed in the following chapter, but it should be obvious from the foregoing discussion that a social process audit that produces useful decision-making data is more likely to be accepted than other kinds of social audits undertaken for punitive or mere public relations purposes. While flirtation with ideological precepts of either a probusiness or an antibusiness bias may be tempting to some social auditors—and while social auditing is generically prone to such ideologically tinged struggles—the final test of social auditing is likely to be whether it is capable of providing insights and understanding not available by other means. Organizational managers will be persuaded to accept it as one more tool in their bag of managerial procedures if it is pragmatically useful. Of all the major types of social auditing so far developed and used, the social process audit has the greatest chance of being that kind of management tool.

A final strength of this particular method of social auditing lies in its flexibility and adaptability to a variety of circumstances and organizational needs. The social process method can be applied to any and all realms of organizational activity, whether they are undertaken voluntarily or required by government regulations, whether related positively or negatively to company profits, whether large-scale or relatively modest in magnitude and expenditure, whether quantifiable or only partially so or not at all, and whether comprising an adjunct "social" program or consisting of a "mainstream" business operation. If an identifiable program or activity exists, if it has detectable social impact or influence, and if there is an organizational determination to analyze its operational effectiveness, then the social process audit technique can be brought to bear. It is the methodology—in other words, the technique—of the social process audit that defines its significance and usefulness as a managerial tool. That methodology and the means of implementing it within an organization are spelled out in the following chapters, as a guide to practical management action.

Some Shortcomings

One of the attractions of the social process audit—indeed, the one that gives it an operational edge over other types—is its acceptance and use, as a guiding framework, of the goals and objectives deemed to be appropriate by the sponsoring organization. This advantage, though, becomes at the same time one of the limitations of this type of social audit. A company may, for example, set goals for its social programs and activities that fall short of public expectations or government standards. Often based on an insufficient knowledge of the complex factors comprising a particular social problem, the company's objectives may be ill-formulated and founded upon false, misleading, or incomplete information. Self-determined program objectives may be simply self-serving. Particularly for companies in the early stages of social analysis and social reporting, where organizational authority for such matters is not clearly delineated and where overall direction is weak or even lacking entirely, program objectives may well emerge as simply reflective of the prevailing organizational distribution of power and influence rather than as goals to be sought for purposes of affecting the company's social climate in positive ways.

While there is no generic reason why the setting of social program objectives need be based upon short-run, socially constrictive, socially negative, or self-serving considerations, various pressures sometimes operate to produce such effects. If that has occurred, then a social process audit that accepts such goals as its criteria will run the risk of perpetuating organizational practices, attitudes, and policies that will be considered unwise and undesirable by some groups within the society. In these cases, social auditors, in order to be professionally responsible, would probably act to render an opinion to the company's management that points out the discrepancy between official program objectives and the social expectations of external groups. Such an opinion then becomes an additional piece of information, which the organization's policy makers can consider in assessing the usefulness of the social audit and the future of the audited activity.

A second kind of limitation of the social process audit also stems from one of its strengths. By focusing upon explicit, discrete programs and activities, the social process audit does not provide the organization's management with a comprehensive view of the total range of social consequences that may result from company operations. Even if a complete inventory of all social effects were to be compiled over time by means of social process audits of individual programs and activities, the analytic results of such audits may not reveal with sufficient clarity the combined social impacts of the organization's activities and practices. In other words, a company's overall social impact may be more than the sum of each area of action examined through social process audits. Such a situation, for example, could conceivably occur where a company's social performance is highly positive and socially beneficial regarding pollution control,

efforts to correct employment discrimination, industrial safety, consumer satisfaction and protection, and legal compliance with antitrust laws, but where the
company's mainstream activity is widely believed to be detrimental to public
health or to be contributory to increasing social complexity, urban congestion
and decay, or worker dissatisfaction.

Closely related to this limitation of the social process audit is another one.
Inasmuch as the criteria for judging program effectiveness are specified by the
organization's management, either directly or by acceptance of criteria defined
by government regulatory agencies, these standards are specific to a given social
program or activity. Standards used to determine whether employment discrimination exists are not useful for making judgments about environmental pollution. The result is that it becomes impossible or highly unlikely for the company's management to be able to make interprogram comparisons of social performance in order to arrive at a rigorously determined judgment about overall
company performance in social matters. There is as yet no yardstick of social
performance—no common denominator—comparable to that used in assessing
economic and financial performance.

If companies are to continue to be brought before the bar of social judgment—and particularly if social evaluation is to be based on social analysis
rather than pure emotion and bias—then this absence of tools for comparison
of interprogram effectiveness will have to be remedied. Such a dilemma cannot
be resolved by reliance upon the discrete, program-by-program analysis represented by the social process audit.

One possible solution to these limitations of the social process audit might
be the further development and refinement of systems of social indicators for
use at national, regional, and local community levels. Such indicators could constitute a framework of overarching criteria against which the performance of
individual organizations could be estimated or perhaps even measured, rather
than relying upon self-determined and self-defined performance criteria. Similarly, an organization might be able to achieve a more comprehensive view of
its overall social impact if the evaluation of individual programs were viewed
within a context of social goals representing broad community consensus, rather
than within the confines of the programs standing alone. Whether there will
ever be developed a common denominator for social performance that will
enable interprogram, intercompany, or interindustry comparisons to be made—
and what that common denominator might be—remains an elusive and unresolved matter.

SOCIAL AUDITING: FUTURE PROSPECTS

Social auditing, even in its early stages and with all of its imperfections,
has already become a viable managerial tool. As the techniques of social meas-

urement are further refined and as work goes forward in such related areas as social indicators, social forecasting, and technology assessment, one can reasonably expect social auditing to become even more useful to organizational policy makers and management decision makers. It is truly an idea and a technique whose time has come.

Three concluding observations about these developments seem to be appropriate in explaining the present and future significance of social auditing.

The major social concerns, problems, and issues that are characteristic of the present are a reflection of genuinely fundamental social changes that have occurred and that continue to occur. These changes include shifts in social attitudes, in social arrangements among groups and classes, and—most importantly— in social values. Many persons have studied and commented on these broad-scale, comprehensive transitions taking place in societies around the globe. It is these fundamental social changes—and not merely fashionable, short-run interests— that motivate, undergird, and sustain professional efforts to develop adequate and accurate tools of social measurement and social evaluation. For that reason, all of these new tools of social technology, including social auditing, will continue to be further developed and refined, as a means of comprehending and coping with the many human problems that arise in the course of widespread social change.

Much has also been written about the contrast and, at times, the conflict between these new social problems and the economic, profit-centered nature of the large-scale corporation. Can we afford to solve our social problems? Must profits be reduced? Who will pay the social costs, and in what proportions? Such questions as these are both troubling and important because they represent one of the many genuine dilemmas of a society in the midst of rapid social transition. If we view the corporation as an economizing institution—that is, as an organization that has achieved a large degree of success in marshaling resources and using them with prudent care and skill—then it is obvious that such institutions are indispensable to the larger social and economic welfare of the society. Such economizing skills are not only to be safeguarded for the greater wellbeing of all but, indeed, they would have to be invented and nourished if they did not already exist. Economizing, which has always been one of the prime responsibilities and skills of professional managers, is a sine qua non of societal life.

The contribution that systematic social evaluation can make to this vital process of organizational economizing is considerable. Social evaluation in all its forms can supplement the tried-and-true methods of measuring an organization's success in attaining suitable levels of economizing. Traditionally, the profit yardstick has been used to measure this success. Now found wanting, as noted at the outset of this chapter, the profit measure needs to be and can be supplemented by information developed by applying new tools of social measurement to organizational performance.

Social auditing, therefore, carries the likelihood of reducing, not exacerbating, the contrast between the economic and social factors involved in organizational operations. The economizing function, so vital to societal well-being, can be more consciously carried out within the larger social context and with an explicit view toward the many social concerns that now characterize our times if organizational decision makers have available the entire array of social, as well as economic, information relevant to their operations. Economizing, far from being threatened by the appearance and adoption of social evaluation techniques, is quite likely to be more fully appreciated and firmly entrenched than ever. Social auditing and the related tools of social measurement are beginning to add a new dimension of knowledge to the task of organizational economizing. That social dimension is vital to a society undergoing a rapid transition of attitudes, practices, and values. Integrated into the economizing process, it holds out the prospect that organizational economizing can simultaneously be preserved as a vital societal function and expanded to include equally vital human and social factors.

A third force that will bring social auditing to the fore as a new management tool is the imperatives of organizational planning. As noted, the socio-politico-economic environment of corporations is changing rapidly. Demands and expectations are rising from all quarters for better, more responsive, and more humane performance. Organizational goals must blend with public expectations to a greater degree than ever before. Only the most careful, comprehensive planning can hope to ensure such results—to achieve an economy of resource usage while serving the multitude of human purposes and needs of society's inhabitants. Strategic planning and policy formulation to achieve these ends are more likely to be successful—in fact, cannot be fully successful in any other way—when systematic social evaluation, undertaken by applying the new tools of social technology, is integrated into the planning and policy process. Social auditing, presently a novel management tool, can play a critical role in the strategic planning and policy systems of large-scale organizations.

For these three reasons—a rapidly changing society that is expected to continue to change, a need to supplement the economizing function of large-scale organizations with social factors reflecting societal expectations, and the imperatives of planning for both economic and social goals—it is therefore reasonable to expect that social auditing will become a permanent feature of the managerial world.

2

PROBLEMS OF THE FIELD

It is fairly easy to form the impression that the main obstacles to social auditing are technical. Leading professional accountants, corporation executives, academic researchers, and hosts of social audit conferees have provided article after article and page after page of discussion focusing on the need for tools to measure social performance. Nearly everyone has concluded that social auditing is a virtually insurmountable task unless or until precise and reliable measurement techniques can be developed.

The trouble with this way of looking at social auditing is that it diverts attention from other, perhaps even knottier and more vexatious, difficulties. There are obstacles to effective social auditing that may be classified as attitudinal, organizational, and political, in addition to the much discussed technical problems and the question of whether or not the procedures traditionally used by accountants can be adapted and utilized for social auditing.

Those problems that might be called attitudinal have to do with the legitimacy of social auditing and social auditors. Attitudes are crucial in this context— the attitudes of managers and their organizations whose social activities will be auditied, the attitudes generated inside the corporation toward social needs and problems as well as toward the social actions perhaps implicit in the very idea of a social audit. Equally important are the attitudes and conventions of the social auditors themselves.

Portions of this chapter appeared in *Business and Society Review*, Autumn 1974, number 11, Copyright 1974, Warren, Gorham, and Lamont, Inc., 210 South Street, Boston, Massachusetts. All rights reserved.

Related to attitudes, but worthy of some individual note, are organizational problems. New organizational devices (or at least ones different from the traditional) are needed to do social audits and to make evaluations. Recognition of these differences by managers responsible for social concerns is necessary. Social concern has to be institutionalized within the organization, rather than being a matter of individual conscience. How this institutionalization is achieved will depend on factors such as whether the company has centralized or decentralized administration and operations, whether its operations are functionally integrated or conglomerate, what type of business it is in (for example, consumer product, manufacturing, transportation, utility, banking, insurance), whether it operates domestically only or also multinationally. And, regardless of the type and scope of its operations, of vital importance is where the organizational authority and responsibility for social matters is located. Within a company or among divisions of a company, there will be both diverse and common social concerns. The treatment of these concerns will depend upon, among other things, where in the organizational structure the responsibility for them is situated.

Outside a company, as well as inside it, political, bureaucratic, and governmental problems arise. There is the basic question of how social standards are created. It may be by decree of a government agency. It may be as a result of public pressure that leads to legislative action. Whatever the process, it is likely to be one of pluralistic negotiation, and legislation or regulation may be established by political muscle rather than by rational means. Business-government relations can be affected, especially the relationships of business with such regulatory agencies as the Federal Trade Commission, the Civil Aeronautics Board, or the Food and Drug Administration.

These attitudinal, organizational, and political problems are exacerbated by, and in turn, exacerbate the technical and methodological problems about which so much has been said and written. There are no social standards about which there is unanimity or, sometimes, even a consensus. Social data do not exist, or if they do, are in a form that the usual quantitative tools cannot measure. The quantitative picture that can be developed does not provide complete social information. Accountants do have some knowledge of measurement techniques that are highly useful, but traditional accounting procedures are concerned with economic values alone (although the Social Measurement Committee of the American Institute of Certified Public Accountants is cognizant of this problem and attempting to deal with it).

Because there are no widely accepted norms and methods of social measurement, the technical problems become attitudinal, organizational, and political as well. It is impossible to separate "the political process and the measuring process....Every time one reports a measurement process there is a halo effect. Whatever one chooses to report will affect people's behavior."[1]

Awareness that the problems associated with social auditing can and do take a variety of forms, many of them of a nontechnical nature, is both necessary and prudent. However, these difficulties are not insurmountable, once they are recognized and understood. A closer examination of each of the problem areas will illustrate that successful passage through and around the attitudinal, organizational, political, and technical shoals is possible, with every likelihood of reaching shore safely and successfully.

ATTITUDINAL PROBLEMS

There is no doubt that tools and techniques for social auditing are needed, and this book describes some of the important ones. But attitudinal difficulties condition and underlie, and sometimes precede, methodological problems. If some company personnel are wary of social auditors, if they look upon social demands and programs as ancillary rather than as functional tasks, their attitudes will differ from those of employees who are committed to social progress. The attitudes of both groups will affect the audit, as will the approach taken by the social auditors themselves as they attempt to gather data.

Deciding What to Audit

A problem preliminary to an actual social audit is deciding what to audit. One reason for the tendency to do social process audits rather than total impact studies is straightforward—and largely attitudinal. Where a comprehensive social audit of a company's overall social performance might be threatening to its officials, particularly if it exposes areas where there should be—but aren't— existing social programs, the social process audit of individual social programs already under way seems less overwhelming, and, practically speaking, more likely to result in usable information.

Once it is agreed that the process audit is the preferred approach, the social auditor and/or the company requesting an audit are faced with another conundrum: What is a "social" program? Do we define as "social" those aspects of business that are not, in theory at least, regulated by the market system? Should social programs be defined in legalistic terms, so that areas and functions for which there are government requirements, such as equal employment opportunity, safety, and pollution, are suitable programs to audit, because there *are* set requirements against which the company can be measured? Or should all programs subject to government regulation be excluded, because the company has to meet government standards and is therefore prepared to do so? Or are these regulated programs nevertheless social, and does simply meeting legal requirements not say enough about the impact of a particular program on workers, customers, and whoever else may be affected by it?

In some cases, "social program" can mean whatever the company believes it should mean, because the company management has the power to say what will or will not be audited and an active interest in finding out more about that particular program. Important discretionary power of definition has, in those cases, been conveyed into the hands of corporate executives. However, in other instances such as equal employment opportunity programs where legislated standards exist and company actions are mandated, it is the government that decides what is a "social program." Having the privilege of deciding what is and what is not a social program and therefore subject to audit is an important prerogative, and the way in which it is exercised reflects the attitudes of the people involved as well as the attitudes embedded in the laws by their proponents and held by those who administer the laws.

Getting Permission to Audit

Not all private corporations are ready to open their doors, let alone their files, to social auditors. Part of their reluctance stems from the sheer novelty of the idea and from the paucity of skilled practitioners. No one wants to be someone's experiment, whether the novice is a hospital intern or a social auditor.

Attitudes toward social auditors and social auditing have ranged all the way from outright hostility and suspicion to open-handed hospitality. Many firms have reportedly adopted a "no outsiders" policy and are determinedly doing their own internal social audits. This approach is not inherently bad, but there is the risk that without an outside view, audits may lose objectivity and drift toward a public relations emphasis. However, this formula has been varied in some firms, with positive results, by bringing in a public accounting firm to lend its expertise and an outsider's objectivity in the data collection, measurement, and reporting phases of the social audit. Still other industrial concerns have taken the "we need all the help we can get" approach and have invited external social auditors to look at their social actions and "tell it like it is."

Quite clearly—and again for reasons easily understood—corporate reactions to the concept of social auditing are mixed, tentative, and hesitant. Some executives and managers may feel that the idea has been imposed upon them externally, by government or by public pressure or by both, and no one is certain of what the results of an audit may mean to the firm or to individuals' jobs.

The important thing to see in all of this is that social auditors may never have to worry at all about the commonly discussed methodological problems unless or until they are allowed onto the corporate premises and given access to relevant information and to the people whose decisions affect the company's relations with society. Getting in the door is the first and most critical attitudinal problem facing the social auditor. For the auditor, it calls for political and social skills first and methodological ones second. For the company manager, what is needed is an attitude of receptivity and a willingness to be convinced, if the case can be made, that a social audit can generate useful information.

Gaining Access to Data

Once inside the company, the social auditor faces a new set of problems. He or she is, first of all, an outsider. Even if a company is doing its own internal audit, the auditors are likely to be drawn from one particular department or even specially assigned for this task, so they may well be strangers to many divi- sions and offices of a company. Unfamiliar with company routines, unknown to all but the few, usually higher-echelon, executives who hired or assigned them, lacking that subtle knowledge of how this company or that division goes about its day-to-day business that is second nature to its veterans, and, perhaps, not being part of the organizational grapevine, the social auditors begin their work in the face of some very real attitudinal difficulties.

Beyond this, social auditors bear a peculiar stigma; their professional work carries a certain moral overtone. They may not speak of the moral aspects of their work, but all who encounter them will suspect that "these people aren't part of our team," because they sometimes insist, contrary to common practice, that explicitly moral and broad societal factors can and should be made an in- tegral part of organizational decision making and activity. Largely for this rea- son, social auditors (external or internal) may even be mistaken for representa- tives of those outside groups that seem to delight in finding and exposing to public gaze various company problem areas. When seen as such, they are not to be trusted, not to be given sensitive data, and to be handled with care and caution by all who are loyal to the organization. Whether these attitudes prevail to the same degree in all companies undergoing social audits is moot, but the potential is there, and social auditors should realize that these attitudes may be encountered.

When a company's social performance is being audited, the chances are that someone or some division is not going to look good. A minority hiring standard was not met. A pollution control record is below legal requirements. A product is proved unsafe or unreliable. These deficiencies may be detected even where a company's overall social record is not bad or even outstanding. Blemishes of this kind may defer a promotion or raise questions that could be- come part of a manager's performance record. In these circumstances, well-known organizational procedures go into motion. Executives may be unavail- able, appointments may be postponed, data may be unobtainable, or the data's clearance may require approval by the unavailable executive.

Clearly, successful social auditors need to be good organizational politicians who can anticipate attitudes that may frustrate their access to data. They need to know where the power is and who wields it. They need to acquire a feel for the fears, anxieties, pressures—and the hopes, rewards, and triumphs—that are part of the everyday life of managers. Most difficult of all, they need to be able to convince people who see them as foes that they can be friends. Social auditors who do not learn to live and breathe the essence of organizational attitudes and politics will not do much auditing, because they won't gain the confidence of those whose performances they are trying to audit. And without the degree of trust, the information needed for the audit will not be forthcoming.

Using the Audit Results

Suppose the first social audit of a company program has been completed, and the audit report is on an executive's desk. What will, or can, he or she do with it?

There are three basic choices. The executive can ignore it or "bury" it, especially if its disclosures are likely to be embarrassing. If, on the other hand, the audit results are positive, the Public Relations Department can be directed to use it to polish the company's image. Or executives can use it as a management tool to raise the level of social awareness and social actions within the company and to control the direction and pace of such social activities. Which of these choices will be made will depend largely upon the attitudes of the executives, as well as on organizational traditions and prevailing social circumstances.

If the audit reveals a social profile of company operations that is more negative than positive, the natural bureaucratic tendencies to ward concealment, judicious doctoring, or discrediting the audit in one way or another may be expected. Faced with an unfavorable report to the Equal Employment Opportunity Commission (EEOC) and possible loss or delay of government contracts, a corporation (or a university or a labor union) is going to put up a strenuous defense and rationalization of its racial and sexual policies. The people responsible for public relations are going to object vociferously to the prospect of citizens' or consumer groups getting an insider's look at a company's dubious safety or pollution record. Top management may well cavil at such public scrutiny.

If the social action story is revealed by the audit to be mixed—some good things and some not so good—there is reason to believe that the company has found a new way to create a favorable image for itself. Moving from five blacks on the payroll to 25 in three years may not satisfy the local human relations commission, but it does allow the company to speak of a fivefold increase, a genuine though perhaps modest advance. Scaling down particulate and chemical emissions by 50 percent may still leave the air too dirty for public health, but the company can legitimately claim that it has begun a difficult task and has the factual proof to demonstrate it. Most executives will be quick to see the advantage of having instituted their own systematic social survey rather than having the story told only by outside agencies more interested in focusing on their own concerns than in worrying about tarnishing the company's image.

The executive's third alternative is one likely to make social auditors, particularly outside ones, feel that their time was well spent. The executive can decide to use the social audit not simply for public relations purposes but as a social tool for modifying the company's influence on society. That can mean, first of all, knowing what social effects the firm is presently creating through its operations. The audit can also reveal any gaps that may exist between a company's social performance and government regulations on such matters as pollution, fair employment, and consumer safety. More important perhaps, these maps of social action, with accompanying cost-benefit ratios if feasible, can give management a more comprehensive understanding of the social terrain and the company's role in it than was previously possible. That in turn can provide a base from which to assess and reformulate the firm's social policies.

Inside the company, the executive may wish to create a continuing social audit for the purpose of monitoring and evaluating the social performance of company divisions and individual managers. Adoption of such a management control system for social policy implementation would be a giant step toward institutionalizing the social function within the company and removing it from the more simple and less effective controls of exhortation and individual conscience. The continuous social audit is likely in the longer run to be seen as a useful training and sensitizing device for managers and employees up and down the line regarding company social policies and programs. This process would have the useful by-product of removing what may be emotion-laden issues from the sphere of individual attitudes—with all of their vicissitudes—to the more stable realm of corporate policy.

ORGANIZATIONAL PROBLEMS

To be a successful management tool, social auditing has to be a flexible technique that is adaptable to a wide variety of circumstances and uses. A wide range of social problems and pressures encountered by large-scale organizations, as well as the organizational diversity that characterizes the corporate world, make flexibility and adaptability imperative.

Social problems and pressures are numerous and diverse, ranging from concern about environmental pollution through various types of employment discrimination to such matters as consumer product safety and effectiveness, worker safety and satisfaction on the job, and equal opportunity for education, housing, transportation, financing, and recreation. Furthermore, public concern over these and other social issues is not evenly distributed throughout the nation. In some communities, the primary focus may be upon educational opportunities. In others, equal access to jobs for all may be uppermost. Moreover, some issues will appear more important at one time period than another. The social scene keeps shifting, placing the emphasis first at one point and then at another, with groups demanding organizational response now in pollution control and next week or next month in housing or jobs.

The problems of diversity are compounded by the presence in the corporate world of several types of organizational patterns or systems. Companies differ greatly regarding (1) the type or types of business they conduct (whether industrial, banking, merchandising, transportation, and so on, or some combination of these); (2) their organizational structure (whether organized by function, by product, by geographic region, or some other way); (3) the geographic and national/cultural extent of their operations (whether local, regional, national, or multinational); (4) the particular organization's traditions regarding social matters (whether open and progressive or closed and defensive); (5) the current attitudes of the organization's leadership group toward social issues and the role to be played by that company; and (6) the type and extent of social legislation confronting the organization, as well as the style and vigor employed by governments in administering such laws.

These twin diversities—of social issues and of organizational patterns—call for a posture of genuine flexibility in choosing organizational activities for social auditing and in applying and implementing both the audit and the audit results. Although the audit *methodology*—that is, the tools and methods—remains essentially the same, regardless of the diverse circumstances in which it is applied, there is nevertheless a need to adapt the method to a variety of conditions. A heavy metals manufacturer (for example, a Bethlehem Steel Corporation) extracting ore from a foreign source will encounter social issues of a different character and magnitude than a consumer products merchandiser (for example, a Sears, Roebuck and Company) selling directly to the public in the United States. Laws, customs, attitudes, the group affected by operations—all of these elements can vary across a wide spectrum.

In the preceding chapter we spoke of the advantages of specific program audits over more comprehensive audits that attempt to assess the total social impact of a single organization. In view of the organizational and social complexities mentioned above, it should now be even more obvious that such comprehensive social audits are difficult if not impossible to conduct and of dubious value even if technically feasible, which appears unlikely at the present time. Social-environmental problems—as with all problems faced by organizational managers—are contextual problems. That is, they are very specific to a given time, place, and social interest. For this reason, social audits and social evaluation generally should be (1) specific to given problems and issues existing at the time or foreseeable at some reasonable time in the future and (2) specific to the particular organization or class of organization and the particular context of problems, attitudes, and laws in which it operates and is expected to operate. When social audits are conducted in this manner, they are likely to produce a type of information that is action oriented and that will therefore be of maximum value to organizational decision makers.

The accompanying matrix illustrates the types and potential numbers of situations and circumstances that could confront a social auditor. The number of possible combinations of factors—both organizational and issue-oriented situations—is impressively large. An "X" placed at any cross-section point within the matrix identifies a situation that is subject to a social audit, as well as indicating some major type of organizational variable to be taken into account in conducting such an audit. The social auditors for Company ABC could, for example, undertake an audit of solid waste pollution associated with the company's operations, but in doing so they would find their auditing activities affected by the type of business conducted by Company ABC, its organizational design (location of authority, incentive systems, and so on), the extent of its operations, and so forth.

Undoubtedly, a great deal more refinement could be built into such a matrix to allow for ever finer distinctions appropriate to a given organization and more specifically related to a given situation at a given point in time. But the matrix even in this generalized form makes the main point that the combination of organizational diversity and issue diversity creates many potentially different audit situations and thereby strongly suggests the need for flexibility and adaptability in social auditing procedures. Once again, we repeat that the social process audit, with its ready acceptance of goals as defined by the organization and its pragmatic outlook, is more likely to exhibit the necessary qualities for successful performance under diverse circumstances than other social audit models.

Institutionalizing Social Evaluation

The major organizational task facing a company that wishes to move forward in developing a positive and active social policy is to "institutionalize" the process of social assessment and social programing.

This means two specific things: (1) to have social problems and social issues regarded by company personnel as normal, typical, and largely enduring characteristics of operations, and (2) to design and establish organizational systems and procedures that will enable the company's decision makers to be informed and to be able to act with regard to social problems that confront the organization. Neither task is easy, but neither is impossible to achieve.

A MATRIX OF SOCIAL AUDIT POSSIBILITIES

Types of Environmental Issues

	Environmental Pollution					Employment Discrimination				Consumer Products			Employee Safety & Satisfaction			etc.
	Air	Wtr	Noise	Rad.	Sol.Wst.	Race	Sex	Age	Relig.	Sfty.	Eff.	etc.	OSHA	Morale	etc.	
Type of Activity																
Industrial																
Banking																
Transportation																
Etc.																
Organizational Structure																
Functional																
Product																
Regional																
Etc.																
Spread of Operations																
Local																
National																
Multinational																
Etc.																
Organizational Traditions																
Closed																
Progressive																
Responsive																
Etc.																
Social Attitudes of the Company																
Pragmatic																
Ideological																
Moderate																
Etc.																
Applicable Social Laws																
Coverage																
Level of gvt.																
Administrative enforcement																
Etc.																

ORGANIZATIONAL VARIABLES

Part of the "institutionalization" is now accomplished fact and not merely a rhetorical demand. In some areas of social concern (for example, employment discrimination, environmental pollution, occupational health and safety, and others), government regulations are in fact making the forceful point that social issues and problems are indeed part and parcel of everyday management operations. Some landmark court rulings of recent years make it painfully obvious that organizations ignore these social realities at considerable risk to their treasuries. Therefore, the process of building social factors into management's consciousness and day-to-day decisions is already well along in its development.

The lag in making social evaluation and effective social programing an integral part of company operations is to be found in the area of organizational design, which, in the case of many companies, has failed to provide adequate budgets, realistic incentivies, a locus of authority and responsibility, and a formal review system for handling social issues on a basis comparable to that applied to economic and financial issues.

These organizational needs have been discussed in some detail in other places.[2] We shall emphasize only their highlights here, in order to stress the point that social auditing can be most successful when it is recognized and implemented as one step in a comprehensive approach to social programing and social policy.

What a company can do to ease its compliance with social legislation and to meet public expectations regarding areas of social concern is to adopt the following types of organizational procedures:

One, sensitize managers at all levels by conducting social impact inventories of various company or divisional operations, including attempts to forecast the reactions (whether positive, negative, or indifferent) of external groups affected by such operations.

Two, apply to social areas the well-established and tested management principles that have worked in economic areas. Specifically, this means the following:

- Setting social goals for the company or division
- Assigning formal responsibility for achieving such goals
- Allocating budgetary resources for these purposes
- Establishing a management control and information system to monitor activities
- Designing and initiating programs and activities to operationalize the social objectives
- Building social factors into the incentive systems of all affected areas of operations
- Assessing the effectiveness of programs and activities through periodic social audits
- Reviewing social policy and social goals at periodic intervals for possible modification.

As others have said, exhortation is no longer sufficient as a realistic approach to corporate social problems. The organization itself—its design, its information flows, its incentives, and the attitudes and actions of its managers—needs to be modified.

It is obviously easier to identify and advocate these changes than to accomplish them. Ackerman reports that the organizations he has studied take from seven to eight years to move from initial perception of a social problem to full organizational commitment and significant organizational change. Each of the actions outlined above may be quite time consuming. Each may have a lower priority for attention from company managers than more urgent matters. Since the entire field of corporate social programing is so relatively new, even the most highly motivated companies are often at a loss to know how to proceed. Where public expectations and social criteria shift rapidly, little confidence can be felt that today's actions will be acceptable to tomorrow's regulators and social pressure groups.

In spite of these very real practical difficulties, the general directions of needed organizational change are becoming more apparent. Corporate social actions will be most effectively undertaken when supported by the same type of organizational system that has proved to be successful in the economic and financial areas. That means clearly delineated authority, realistic budgetary allocations, operational goals and programs, and incentives to achieve results. When social programing is seen as a management problem and subjected to the same systematic treatment given to other types of company operations, progress can be expected to follow as night follows day. Such a managerial posture toward the social arena can be fully effective only when accompanied by the needed organizational modification.

POLITICAL PROBLEMS

It cannot be said too often that social auditing is not an entirely rational undertaking. Its practitioners may believe themselves to be precise and objective. They may employ the latest and most sophisticated tools of analysis. They may adopt all of the familiar scientific paraphernalia to reduce the intrusion of their own personal biases and prejudices. But in the end, it must be acknowledged that they are themselves human and therefore subject to all of the irrationalities and subjective biases of their society. In addition, they are doing the auditing for other human beings who are equally subject to the same irritational pulls and tugs of the social system. No one is totally disinterested in the outcome of a social audit—not the auditor, the persons commissioning it, or the interest groups affected by it.[3]

Perhaps as important, social auditors do their auditing in a context of political and governmental institutions. Few would argue that politics and governmental processes are an instance of pure reason. Along with the psychological and social subjectivities just mentioned, a significant number of irrationalities arise from the political system. All of these irrational elements appear to be inherent in the social—and particularly the political—processes that surround social auditing activities. There is no way for the social auditor to escape the influence of these subjective and irrational occurrences. Acknowledging that they exist is, however, one way to put social auditing on a realistic basis.

These social (and very human) complications of social auditing arise from a number of explicit sources. One such source is to be found in the demands of various social pressure groups. Whether they are irate consumers or workers aggrieved by unsafe working conditions, conservationists pleading for preservation of the wilderness or conservationists advocating the plowing up of that wilderness to obtain scarce energy resources, women demanding equal treatment with men or American Indians demanding that old treaties be respected—in any and all such cases, the grievances, the frustrations, the accumulated anger and hostility are scarcely ever calculated to result in a carefully reasoned, unemotional statement of the issues. Quite the contrary, the case is often (perhaps even deliberately) overstated, as a ploy in the bargaining leading up to some negotiated settlement. Such tactics can elicit equally angry and emotional responses from the groups who are the target of the dissidents, further complicating and exacerbating the entire matter.

In these familiar circumstances, irrationalities abound. A social pressure group, in the heat of the moment and carried along by the momentum and the tactics of the struggle, may not accurately perceive what is in its own best interest. A fair degree of technological ignorance may exist, particularly in such complex areas of social concern as environmental pollution. Fears may outrun reason. Demands for corrective action may result in economically, politically, technologically, and socially unrealistic goals and compliance deadlines. A given social pressure group may well fail to perceive its interests within the larger social, political, economic, and technological context from which a negotiated settlement will come. One result, regardless of the eventual outcome, is an accumulation of irrationalities. The social auditor must be alert to them. They will condition the methods and outcome of the audit.

Still other irrational factors stem from the pluralistic negotiation process that leads to new or modified social regulatory legislation. All of the emotion-laden beliefs, demands, and reactions mentioned above pour into the legislative process as a social demand moves from initial formulation to drafted bill and eventually to enacted law.[4] A similar process affects the evolution of executive orders. The courts, though better insulated, are not immune to the social clamor of the moment. Legislated or mandated social criteria may therefore be unrealistic or technologically unattainable, particularly if accompanied by inflexible compliance deadlines. The necessary technology may not be available to carry out the spirit, not to mention the letter, of the law within the time specified.

Expertise may not yet be developed or it may be in short supply. Added to these difficulties is the fact that many social problems now plaguing us are newly emerging ones, with new and changing dimensions. Concern in recent years about such chemicals as polyvinylchloride, aerosol propellants, and nitrous oxides, among others, is a case in point. Seldom are all such considerations reflected in new social regulations, laws, and court orders, so rapidly does the horizon of social concern and scientific knowledge move. For the organization subject to these new social regulations, compliance is obviously made more difficult by these irrationalities. Where mandated goals, compliance criteria, and performance evaluation are shot through with such unevenness, the task of the social auditor becomes more complex, requiring political sensitivity of a high order.

A third source of irrationality that surrounds social auditing is in the administrative agencies of government that require social reporting on a wide range of activities. These agencies are themselves human and political organizations, subject to the inefficiencies and bureaucratic routines of all organizations. Due to the budgetary niggardliness of legislative bodies, regulatory agencies are often understaffed and unable to respond in timely fashion, sometimes lacking in sufficient experience and expertise (particularly in those areas where the knowledge and expectation horizon moves rapidly), and inherently at odds with the companies they regulate, thus leading to mistrust and lack of confidence on the part of the regulated. In addition, political pressures from one side or the other may be brought to bear upon the agency by legislators or by members of the executive branch. At times, competing, contradictory, or overlapping regulatory jurisdictions may exist. Until recent changes, the role of the Atomic Energy Commission as both promoter and safety regulator of nuclear power plants, along with the subordinate and weaker regulatory role of the Environmental Protection Agency, was cited as such an example of overlapped and unclear jurisdictional authority. Due to understaffing and organizational inertia, it is quite possible that new social concerns may emerge at a faster pace than the proper regulatory agency can handle them. The Food and Drug Administration, as well as the Consumer Product Safety Commission, have at times found themselves in such a situation. As a result of all of these (perhaps inherent) characteristics of the regulatory process, the instructions and expectations emenating from the administrative agencies may not be clear, creating hesitation and uncertainty for the reporting company. Once again, the social auditor needs to know of these uncertainties if the audit is to proceed in the proper directions and if it is to produce results that are useful to a sometimes harrassed management group.

Still another source of irrationality that affects social auditing is apparent in the very process of organizational decision making. The rational measurement and reporting of social performance may (and usually does) compete with other factors that are important to the decision makers and vital to their individual survival within the organization. One expert in social evaluation has this to say about policy makers and decision makers in organizations:

> They are members of a policy-making system that has its own values and its own rules. Their model of the system, its boundaries and pivotal components, goes far beyond concern with program effectiveness. Their decisions are rooted in all the complexities of the democratic decision-making process: the allocation of power and authority, the development of coalitions, and the trade-offs with interest groups, professional guilds, and salient publics. How well a program is doing may be less important than the position of the congressional committee chairman, the political clout of its supporters, or other demands on the budget. A considerable amount of ineffectiveness may be tolerated if a program fits well with prevailing values, if its satisfies voters, or if it pays off political debts.[5]

Although this comment was made with respect to attempts to evaluate publicly financed programs of government agencies, its logic can be applied with equal validity to private organizations. All organizational decision makers, whether in the public or private sector, do, in fact, pay heed to their survival and official tenure. That means, among other things, that their own values and those of the organization—whether consistent or at odds with the values of various pressure groups—will have a higher appeal than others. It also means that the company's key decision makers will respond to implicit, embedded organizational goals and routines not readily apparent to the social auditor or to any outsider. To the casual or even the careful observer, they will seem to be marching to a different drummer. This muffled organizational cadence is the drumbeat of individual survival, more important to the insider than the outsider. And, finally, there is a need to demonstrate *acceptable* achievement for the organization, regardless of the *real* outcome. A person well attuned to the nuances of an organization and the values of its primary policy makers may prove to be much more interested in satisfying the needs and demands arising from those sources than in responding to the results of a rationally conducted social audit. It may be true, for example, that compliance with an EEOC guideline or time table for minority employment is of subordinate importance to having it *appear* that the organization is moving toward compliance, whether in fact any significant progress is being made. Such is the (irrational) stuff of which an individual's organizational survival is often made. So it may be true that a system of rational social reporting is submerged by such dictates. A social auditor should know such possibilities.

Not least among the sources of irrational action confronting the social auditor are the demands that political and professional career building may inject into the arena of social problem solving. Politicians must move with the times and the issues. To fail to do so is to court political oblivion. While some political figures have provided useful and wise leadership in areas of social concern, others have allowed their enthusiasm for given issues and their voter sensitivities to outrun their sense of political statesmanship. Under these circumstances, social abuses and problems may well be exaggerated for political effect, pressures for hasty and ill-considered action may become irresistible, unrealistic compliance deadlines and performance criteria may be advocated and made a part of regulatory legislation, and in general a sort of political grandstanding may replace an emphasis upon the need for a careful, systematic approach to complex social and environmental issues. At times, such political antics are accompanied by a type of social-issue camp follower, the instant professional consultant who, with inadequate social knowledge but consummate salesmanship skills, may convince a company that finds itself under severe social pressures of one kind or another that he is their savior, at least for the moment. Where the problem-solving climate is often so fraught with uncertainty and where non-compliance with social demands or government regulations may be costly to the organization, such disguised bromides have their appeal. All of this is simply to acknowledge in still another way that where these kinds of career-building behaviors occur, the task of the social auditor is made that much more difficult and complicated.

Social auditing is indeed complicated—but not made impossible—by all of these political and social irrationalities. A foreknowledge of their potential impact on the social auditor and the social audit itself is important. There is no point in trying to escape their influence or, as some would do, in pretending that such irrational forces don't exist or can be safely ignored. The successful social auditor builds upon the knowledge that social measurement and social reporting are performed in a sociopolitical climate, filled with all of the irrationalities and frailities of the human persons and the human institutions whose activities are being audited and reported.

Since the social process audit accepts the goals and objectives set by the organization's management for its social activities, it is the audit method that is more likely to reveal the actual factors that are of greatest interest to the decision makers and thereby to produce information of maximum acceptability and usefulness to them.

> Perhaps one of the reasons that [social] evaluations are so readily disregarded is that they address only official goals. If an evaluator also assessed a program's effectiveness in meeting political goals... he might learn more about the measures of success that decision-makers value....

And:

> It does appear that evaluation research is most likely to affect decisions when the researcher accepts the values, assumptions,

and objectives of the decision-maker. This means, obviously, that decision-makers heed and use results that come out the way they want them to. But it suggests more than the rationalization of pre-determined positions. There is a further, important implication that those who value the *criteria* that evaluation research uses, those who are concerned with the achievement of official program goals, will pay attention as well. The key factor is that they accept the assumptions built into the study. Whether or not the outcome results agree with their own wishes, they are likely to give the evidence a hearing. But evaluation results are not likely to be persuasive to those for whom other values have higher priority.[6]

In other words, because social auditing is beset by social, organizational, and political complexities, its greatest chance for successful use as a management tool lies in recognizing these complicating factors and adapting measurement and reporting methods accordingly.

TECHNICAL PROBLEMS

At a time when the science of physical measurement can create a clock in Boulder, Colorado, that is accurate to one second in 300,000 years, the measurement of the effect of social actions is, at best, reminiscent of the [old television quiz show] ...and its question "Is it larger than a breadbox?" In fact, most social measurement is nowhere as useful for the intended purpose.[7]

When those interested in social auditing gather together, questions about social measurement invariably arise. Those that get the most attention are (1) Is it possible to measure social factors with an acceptable degree of precision?; and (2) What standards will be used to judge the social performance of corporations? Both matters are complex, and discussions of them tend to bristle with such exotic phrases as "utiles," "pareto optima," "consensual norms," "cost-benefit analysis," and "independent attest function."

One result of these discussions is the creation of the erroneous impression that measurement problems are purely technical matters better left to experts who speak the language of mathematics, economics, and accounting. However, a closer look reveals a different story.

Measurement problems tend to be related to questions of definition and identification, two factors that can—and usually do—permit wide-ranging individual interpretation. Consider, for example, the definition of the goals of a social program. A social auditor looking at a program within a company may well find that the chief executive officer has one set of goals and sees the program fulfilling one particular purpose, while the manager and employees of the department administering the program view it differently. The government may see yet another purpose for the program, and the people (inside or outside the company) who are affected by the program will obviously have still different goals for it. Whose goals, then, should the social auditor consider in the attempt to, first, identify the *program's* goals and, second, evaluate whether or how the goals are being achieved? The answer is probably that the goals of everyone concerned should be examined, but if this is the case, how should the goals be weighted when the time comes to evaluate the program's effectiveness? Should the president's goals be considered more important than those of the recipients of the program's benefits? Goals have a personal and subjective dimension as well as a social and organizational meaning, and they are vitally important in any attempt to measure a program's effectiveness. Efforts to apply traditional measurement and weighting systems inevitably involve the consideration of individualized and nonobjective factors.

Definitional problems, too, affect attempts to quantify, standardize, and measure. Terminology that has one unquestioned meaning in traditional financial or economic contexts may be misunderstood, misconstrued, misleading, or simply inappropriate when it is applied to situations other than those for which it was formulated. There has been enough discussion about whether or not "social auditing" is a legitimate term to make this point clear. If "auditing" is to mean strictly what it means in accounting terminology, then we may be a long way from "social auditing"; indeed, in those terms, it may be impossible to do. If, however, the term takes on a different meaning in a different context, "social auditing" is being done. These terminology problems become attitudinal difficulties when they lead to dissension about whether "social auditing" is or is not—or should be—"auditing." If it is auditing, should accountants be the only people who do it? If it is not auditing in the traditional sense—or should not be—what is it, whose ground rules should be used, what standards should be applied? These two examples indicate clearly that while there are genuine methodological problems and dilemmas, measurement is inextricably intertwined with political, social, and attitudinal issues.

Whose Standards Should Be Used?

Consider the question of the criteria to be used in judging a corporation's social performance. Whose standards should prevail respecting air pollution? Those of an aroused citizen group? Of the Environmental Protection Agency? Of scientists testifying for the polluting industry or of those who testify against it? Of employees who may lose their jobs if the plant is forced to shut down? Or should profit-oriented stockholder values prevail?

Not only will this conflict be resolved through the process of bargaining and negotiation (a political process), but the outcome will represent some compromise of the positions and viewpoints of various parties. The technical measurement experts ask the question "Whose values will constitute the criteria for corporate performance?" with an air of despair, as if there is no answer. True, there is no pristine answer, free from the pulling and hauling of everyday problems, and the outcome might not be as neatly packaged as one would like. Criteria may be arbitrary, shifting, and difficult to quantify precisely. But from the negotiating process, some standards do emerge. Ambient air standards now exist, representing a compromise of the views of many interested groups. The same can be said for minority employment standards, for product safety standards, for drug effectiveness standards, and for standards in other areas of social concern.

What Should Be Measured and How?

Deciding what and how to measure are also questions of value choices. Since none of us exists in a social or political vacuum, those choices about what is worth measuring are inevitably affected by sociopolitical factors.

What do you identify as racial or sexual discrimination? You can compute the numbers of jobs held by minority persons and compare those figures with jobs held by the dominant majority, and such measures are important to make. But what about the more subtle factors such as racial and sexual attitudes, feelings, deep-seated prejudices? Many social factors simply cannot be stated or measured in quantitative terms, or the figures that can be developed do not really capture the essence of the problem. One way out of this dilemma is to design meaningful nonquantitative measures that will allow comparisons to be made. Another possibility is to find ways to state qualitative factors in quantitative terms. Some encouraging developments are under way now to design "social indicators" that will help measure a community's social well-being, just as various "economic indicators" are used to help calculate economic well-being. (Some of these approaches are described in Chapter 1.)

Assuming that adequate social measuring sticks can be developed, one encounters the further problem of deciding which criteria to use in assessing a company's social performance. What is the standard of social "good" or "bad"? For example, how many blacks must be hired before a company or a union is nondiscriminatory? Should the number be equal to their proportion in the general population? Or to the population in the particular community in which the social audit is being made? Or should employment opportunities be made even greater than either of these percentage figures, as a way of compensating today's blacks for the long history of discrimination? Similar difficulties arise in the case of women. Because women constitute more than half of the population, is any company guilty of sexual discrimination if the majority of its employees are male? If a percentage figure is used, for blacks or women, should it be a percentage of the total employee force, in all ranks and all jobs? Or should the figure be divided by job classification and rank, for both blacks and women?

In these examples as well as in others that could be cited, social auditors need generally accepted social standards against which to measure, but these standards frequently do not exist, or data that do exist may not be usable to reach any kind of consensus on social criteria. Here, too, help may come as current research on the development and application of social indicators goes forward.

Clearly, even deciding *how* to measure social elements—a decision that would seem, at first glance, to be just as technical as it can be—is a process that reflects philosophic attitudes and points of view. When Abt Associates set out to convert social costs and benefits into dollars, there was a storm of protest from those who said it couldn't—and/or shouldn't—be done. There are values in life that are not reducible to such crass calculations, claimed some of the critics. Others maintained that Abt's dollar figures give an incomplete and misleading rundown on a company's social posture. Closely allied to this view is the one that maintains that social auditing has the same dim future enjoyed by all attempts to attach numbers to the values that are important to individuals and to society. Welfare economists who have attempted for years to quantify the fugitive elements of "preference," "utility," and "indifference" have taken their share of criticism for even making the attempts. On the other side of the controversy are those who urge that progress lies in the direction of quantifying everything. Their attitude tends to be that if measures don't exist now, we should get on with the job of designing them.

What these conflicting positions tell us in that measurement, even in its most technical manifestations, is very much a political, philosophical, and "human" undertaking. Virtually all corporate actions have economic and social results and involve large numbers of people from different groups. Each group may feel more strongly about one issue than another, leading to immense difficulties in comparing different areas of social action and concern. It is difficult, if not impossible, to find a standard of comparison applicable to, for example, industrial pollution and employment discrimination. The net result is that moral, ethical, and political problems emerge as equally important to technical problems, and the latter may become the former. The prevailing sociopolitical structure and process exert great influence upon the measurement enterprise by helping to decide whose values will be used as criteria, what social elements will be measured, and how the measurement will be done.

Methodological Problems

All of the foregoing is not to imply that there are not genuine methodological problems associated with social auditing. The literature abounds with descriptions of attempts to develop measurement and reporting methods that will be useful and accurate (see Chapter 1). And for every article outlining a proposed measurement system, there is a response indicating the reasons why that system will not work. A number of examples will illustrate these methodological dilemmas.

What indicators should be used in attempts to measure the effects of pollution? Tons of pollutants? Number of days the plant had to shut down because the air pollution level in the area was too high? Dollar cost to others of either the pollution or the shut-downs? The Environmental Protection Agency has set standards, but perusal of the daily newspapers in any large city shows clearly that not everyone agrees with or abides by these criteria. The standards that are set may not be accurate indicators. A plant may have no shut-down days at all and still be a high polluter; if it is the only plant in the area, the total level of air pollution in that area may never reach the stage where shut-down is required. But this is no measure of what the plant is doing that causes pollution or what it is doing to prevent pollution.

Suppose a corporation wants to evaluate the ways in which it attempts to improve the quality of life for its employees. The company's goal might be identified as a desire to provide a positive work environment and to enhance the quality of life in the corporation's entities. One step in this direction, it might be decided, is to improve the lighting in the plants. Does this plan, when it is effected, help meet the goal? There are various elements to be evaluated, some of which are measurable and some not.

In this example, it may be possible to measure directly some effects but not others. How much the lighting in a plant has been improved is measurable quantitatively, but what this improvement means to the workers may not be. One can measure the input—what changes in lighting occurred—and, perhaps, an output—increased worker productivity, for example, if there is such an increase. The output may be an effect of the input and may well be measurable, at least in part. But, if an attempt is being made to measure ways in which the corporation is thereby improving the quality of working life, there are other effects that should be measured. These could be called perceived effects (for example, the workers' reactions to and feelings about the improved lighting) that are not easily measurable, if at all.

Even factors that seem relatively simple to measure may turn out to have hidden difficulties. Consider the area of plant safety and reduction of accidents. This seems to be an easy area to measure because accidents are identifiable; they must be reported and tabulated, and the Occupational Safety and Health Administration has definite requirements for these reports. But, to what extent are all accidents really reported? Are there some incidents that are not entered in the statistics? Are the official definition of an accident and the workers' perceptions one and the same? What was actually reported? Was the accident reported the one that really occurred?

Another quantification technique that has generated a flurry of interest is human resource accounting, in which a firm attempts to measure the cost and value of people to the organization. Items normally considered to be expenses, such as employee training and benefits, are treated as investments that contribute to building up resources. In terms of social benefits, the idea of seeing human resources as assets may bolster employees' morale. In speeches, in internal publications, and even in annual reports, executives frequently say something to the effect that "our employees are our most valuable resources and assets." But until the recent attempts at human resource accounting, these valuable resources and assets never appeared in a financial statement. So there may well be some social value (at the least, in a public relations sense; at best, in the company's truly perceiving and treating employees as assets) in human resource accounting.

The technical problem with trying to put human resources into the balance sheet as an asset is that these resources have no separate existence of their own, as do a patent or trademark or a piece of equipment or property. The Coca Cola formula and trademark, for example, would have value to another organization and could be sold for a set dollar amount. The labor force does not necessarily perform functions that would be conveyable or salable by the company. In addition, human assets could take a sudden decline in value that could not be forecasted or systematically depreciated.

Various attempts have been made, by David Linowes and others, to construct accounting systems to measure social data. But these systems may leave out some important information. Truthful and informative marketing and advertising practices are very positive socially, but it could be extremely difficult to put an identifiable cost figure on them when compared with misleading or false advertising. Another problem with some proposed systems of social measurement is the danger of misunderstanding, misinterpretation, and negativism.

> ...a company with superb engineering might design its pollution-control procedures to increase the efficiency of its production technology to the point that better pollution control costs little or nothing. A company with poorer technical ability would be perceived as making a contribution because its pollution-control apparatus yielded a net loss. Or an entire industry might, by virtue of its technology, appear to be more (or less) socially responsible depending on how efficiently its technology permitted it to handle pollution.[8]

The point is that social reporting must guard against measuring only deficiencies. When this happens, the report becomes a negative document saying, in effect, "Why haven't you solved the whole problem?" rather than indicating progress that has been made. This approach runs the risk of making the whole concept of social auditing seem negative, critical, and carping. The objections raised may be similar to those sometimes voiced about the "management by exception" technique in which a manager's performance is evaluated, and only those items or ratios that are unfavorable receive attention.

Accenting the Positive

It is clear that those who bemoan the difficulties of social measurement are not merely attempting to bury the social audit or to avoid the other problems associated with it. There are real and serious methodological and technical difficulties. But selective information about selected areas is available or able to be generated, as in the areas of pollution control, occupational safety and health, and employment discrimination, and work on social indicators is proceeding rapidly. As time goes on, existing information and criteria may be altered, strengthened, or more clearly delineated and defined. Government, corporate, and public consensus may be reached about measurements in some areas considered to be of national importance. Companies have already begun to try social audits of program areas that are of particular importance or interest to the company, its workers, or its community, or about which management needs and wants some systematic information, whether it be quantitative or qualitative, objective or subjective, or some combination.

The difficulties are real and must be recognized, but they should not be used as excuses for not proceeding. The more social auditing is tried, using a variety of methods, the more likely social auditors are to find their way through the maze of measurement problems, to recognize the attitudinal, organizational, and political implications of such problems, and to realize that if we cannot make our way through the morass, perhaps we ought to be looking for a way around it—for alternatives to traditional measurement as tools for social auditing.

ACCOUNTING AND SOCIAL AUDITING

There is little in the present accounting and reporting systems of corporations that enables anyone to determine whether corporations have well-formulated sets of goals for social performance, or to measure the extent of progress toward realization of these goals.[9]

These are not the words of social scientists who are opposed to quantification, nor do they emanate from a disenchanted, antiestablishment activist group. This statement was made by the Research and Policy Committee of the Committee for Economic Development, a prestigious, business-oriented, and, in large part, business-supported organization. It is not meant to be condemnatory, but it identifies an issue that must be considered when the role of accounting in the social auditing process is raised.

In its definition of accounting, the authoritative Accounting Principles Board (now the Financial Accounting Standards Board) of the American Institute of Certified Public Accountants also indicates clearly just what the generally accepted scope of accounting is.

> Accounting is a service activity. Its function is to provide quantitative information, primarily financial in nature, about economic entities that is intended to be useful in making economic decisions....
> Financial accounting for business enterprises is one branch of accounting. It provides...a continual history quantified in money terms of economic resources and obligations of a business enterprise and of economic activities that change these resources and obligations.[10]

The meaning is clear. The purposes and values of accounting have been derived from an "economic-purpose" institutional context. They focus upon accounting for economic values within a profit system, and they focus upon the activities of individual companies. Social auditors, however, attempt to measure more than economic factors and are concerned with factors other than profit alone. The social actions they want to measure and report on are broader, more diverse, and more complex phenomena than those dealt with in standard accounting procedure. In addition, financial measures may be inapplicable or nonuseful.

Does this disparity mean that there is no role for accounting in social auditing? An affirmative answer to this question would be foolish, for there is much to be gained from a partnership. Accounting information is an important part of management decision making and control systems, and it is to be hoped that the day approaches when social information, too, will be used for managerial decision making, planning, and forecasting.

Accounting technology includes well-known and tested methods of calculation, measurement, classification, and reporting, as well as the numerical logic and discipline that guide the use of these methods. Some of this measurement technology should and probably can be extracted from its conventional institutional context for use in an expanded social setting. For example, the question of social costs is one that a number of proposed systems attempt to grapple with. While there are real difficulties in attempting to apply traditional accounting cost theory to social factors, Professor Neil Churchill of Harvard and others as well are conducting research in this area, hoping to develop a modified cost-benefit approach that can be applied to social measurement. Human resource accounting is another attempt, already under way in some organizations, to apply generally accepted accounting principles to elements that, in the past, have not been included in financial statements. David Linowes, a CPA whose proposed Socio-Economic Operating Statement is described in Chapter 1, would like to see interdisciplinary teams, captained by CPAs, drawing up such statements.

Whether or not these attempts will be successful is not the most critical point here. What is important is that many accountants believe that their profession can, should, and must enter this new domain of social measurement and social accounting. Arthur Toan, chairman of the Social Measurement Committee of the American Institute of Certified Public Accountants, believes that accountants are and will be involved in social measurement by accident, by desire, and by concern. Most information presently compiled about company activities is drawn up by accountants or prepared in accordance with accounting standards, so it is natural to think of accountants in connection with the preparation of corporate reports. Accountants prepare the financial statements that appear in annual reports, corporate directories, and government reports; shouldn't their experience and training be drawn upon in the preparation of nonfinancial statements for these same media? Nonfinancial experts hold no patent on concern about social issues. Shouldn't accountants be able to express their own social concerns by contributing their professional expertise to efforts that support those concerns?

The primary role of accountants is usually one of attestation and verification of information. They design and establish financial measurement systems, they organize and compile the data that are fed into these systems, and they verify the information produced by the systems. They are accustomed to gathering, organizing, and presenting data for both managerial and external (for example, stockholder, government) interests. Where these activites can contribute to the development of social information systems, accountants may have a great deal to offer.

However, accounting technology has its limitations, which should be borne in mind along with the contributions it can make. Accounting is not the most precise science of measurement we have, as many accountants have acknowledged, admitting that subjective determinations are made in such areas as research and development costs and price-earnings ratios and even going so far as to say that "neither precision nor total accuracy are possible in economic terms."[11] So social auditors should be wary of attempts to develop precise measuring systems, because if precision cannot be achieved completely in financial accounting, it is even less likely to be possible in social accounting.

Another difficulty may lie in the very existence of generally accepted accounting principles and forms. Accountants and those with whom they work will have to beware of trying to gather data in ways that will fit into existing systems to report new types of data.

Any effort toward a standardized social accounting model will have to be interdisciplinary, a necessity agreed upon by nearly all—accountants and non-accountants alike—who have discussed this topic. In the past, accounting has borrowed from the measurement concepts of engineering and economics, as well as of algebra and other branches of mathematics. Now the field must be willing to consider the concepts and constructs of sociology, psychology, anthropology, law, political science, and other fields as well.

A number of accountants have indicated their awareness and acceptance of the need to open the doors of their field to new and different ideas. Some have gone so far as to admit that quantification, as that term is ordinarily used, may be impractical and/or impossible for some forms of social information. R. Lee Brummet, writing about "Nonfinancial Measures in Social Accounting," believes that "accountants are becoming more tolerant of a degree of 'messiness' in their quantification efforts."[12] Still others agree that quantification may not be either necessary or appropriate for social reporting, although most interested accountants are working toward systems that will be compatible with standard financial reporting practices. They believe that information presented in accepted, standardized formats gains more credibility inside and outside the corporation. There may be some legitimacy to their beliefs, and it is true that accountants usually have the attention and respect of managers, but at one time, standard accounting and reporting forms were as new and unknown as social reporting procedures are today. All the more reason for a partnership that brings to social auditing that accounting expertise and those procedures that— combined with the expertise and procedures provided by those who have studied social problems—will lead to the best possible social reporting.

NOTES

1. Justin Davidson in American Institute of Certified Public Accountants, *Social Measurement: Points of View of Sociologists, Businessmen, Political Scientists, Government Officials, CPAs* (New York: American Institute of Certified Public Accountants, 1972), p. 38.

2. See Robert Ackerman, "How Companies Respond to Social Demands," *Harvard Business Review*, July-August 1973; and David H. Blake, "The Management of Corporate Social Policy," a lecture presented at the Frederick R. Kappel Symposium on Corporate Social Policy: Formulation, Implementation, and Measurement, College of Business Administration, University of Minnesota, May 10, 1974.

3. See Ian I. Mitroff, *The Subjective Side of Science* (Amsterdam: Elsevier Scientific Publishing Company, 1974).

4. See Robert L. Peabody et al., *To Enact a Law* (New York: Praeger Publishers, 1972).

5. Carol H. Weiss, "Where Politics and Evaluation Research Meet," *Evaluation* no. 3 (1973): 40.

6. Ibid., pp. 40, 41.

7. Stewart D. McElyear, "Auditing Corporate Social Impact in a Period of Rising Social Concern," in Meinolf Dierkes and Raymond A. Bauer, eds., *Corporate Social Accounting* (New York: Praeger Publishers, 1973), p. 309.

8. Raymond A. Bauer, "Commentary on 'Let's Get on With the Social Audit,'" *Business and Society Review*, Winter 1972-73, p. 44.

9. Committee for Economic Development, *Social Responsibilities of Business Corporations* (New York: CED, 1971), p. 48.

10. Accounting Principles Board, American Institute of Certified Public Accountants, Section 1023, Statements .01 and .02, October 1970.

11. See, for example, David Linowes, "Let's Get on with the Social Audit," *Business and Society Review*, Winter 1972-73, p. 41; and John C. Burton, "An Educator Views the Public Accounting Profession," *Journal of Accountancy*, September 1971, p. 51.

12. In Dierkes and Bauer, eds., op. cit., p. 350.

3

THE CONTENT OF
A SOCIAL PROCESS
AUDIT

The problems confronting social auditing are immense and not easily resolved. However, the most severe difficulty is that of faint-heartedness when technical and organizational problems are allowed to interfere with efforts to go beyond the "good idea—but..." stage into the "let's see what we can do" stage. With the intention of providing support and encouragement as well as a possible model for those willing to see what can be done, we set forth in this and succeeding chapters a method that has been used to assess several social programs in a *Fortune* 500 firm.

Based on our experience, we will discuss in a step-by-step fashion an approach or method for the conducting of a social process audit. We do not claim that this systematic approach to undertaking a social process audit is the best or the only one, but it *is* a method that has been used. It has survived the test of actual implementation, though not without some revisions. Moreover, the method developed, and its underlying philosophy, can serve as a starting point for others to conduct their own social process audit. Thus, the approach presented here is by no means the only approach; it is instead an approach that may be of value in taking the social process audit tool off the conceptual shelf and putting it into the hands of managers who are aware of the need to evaluate their social programs.

While the discussion that follows seeks to examine a generally useful model, it must be emphasized that this approach should be adapted to a specific social program being evaluated. Moreover, some adjustments will be necessary to ensure the appropriateness and sensitivity of the model to specific organizations. The point is that the model to be examined cannot be lifted from these pages and immediately be applicable to the precise needs of the manager. Some adjustment and adaptation may be necessary, but this can be done easily within the context of the method presented here.

Before beginning this examination, though, it is important to say once again that a social process audit is designed to evaluate specific social programs established by management. Moreover, it evaluates the programs in the light of managerial or corporate goals and objectives. The technique of social process auditing does not assess the overall social impact of the corporation nor does it judge management according to some preconceived notion of what is good or correct behavior. Instead, the social process audit and the operational approach discussed here seek to analyze specific programs in terms of the goals established for the program, the resources committed to the program, the mechanisms by which the program is implemented and managed, and finally the results of the program. Thus, the social process audit is a dynamic technique that goes far beyond a kind of bottom-line approach to evaluation and managerial control. It seeks to provide managers with a technique that will enable them to determine whether the program is being implemented effectively, how it can be improved, and generally whether the program is worthy of continuation according to their particular standards.

A MODEL FOR CONDUCTING A SOCIAL PROCESS AUDIT

Program History and Description

While the social process audit is concerned with the evaluation of a social program at a specific point in time, it is useful to have some knowledge about the general nature of the program and its historical antecedents and evolution. Obtaining initial summary information about the program enables the analyst to have a broad view of the program. This is important since subsequent auditing steps focus on specific parts of the effort and its implementation, and in the absence of an overall view, the auditor might fail to observe the important relationships that exist. Moreover, general information about the program aids in the identification and formulation of questions to be asked, data to be collected, and a specific auditing strategy to be pursued.

Historical material about the beginnings of the program may be helpful in determining the initial goals of the program as well as the conditions and factors that led to company involvement. Information about the early years of the program may provide insights into the historical antecedents of current practices and objectives. For example, once appropriate objectives or procedures may be dysfunctional in the present, but historical analysis may reveal why and how these practices were established, and thus how they can be changed. After determining why a program was initially developed, questions could then be focused on whether these earlier conditions still exist; whether the program substantively and procedurally has adapted to the changed circumstances; or whether it is simply a matter of doing things the way they have always been done. In short, present goals and operations can be better understood in the historical context of the program. Consequently, historical information about goals, inputs, management, and achievements of the program may be useful in the current evaluation of the program. Specific types of useful information will be discussed as we proceed with an examination of how to conduct a social process audit.

Goals of the Program

Analysis and assessment of program goals is crucial to the social process audit, particularly since there is much evidence to indicate that the objectives of corporate social programs are often ill-defined. While the process audit does not seek to pass judgment as to the rightness or wrongness of a corporate goal, it must nevertheless be concerned about program goals and the goal-setting process. Information about goals is critical for a number of reasons. Most fundamentally, the social process audit technique evaluates the effectiveness of a program in terms of the corporation's own objectives. Secondly, the assessment of the resources committed to the program and the effectiveness of program implementation are considered in relation to the goals established by management. In other words, corporate objectives for special social programs serve as the benchmarks to be used in the social process audit technique.

The first step in goal analysis of this sort involves the identification of the goals. This is a difficult but obviously necessary task. The analyst should be alert to the precision or lack of precision in goal definition. Moreover, there may be high or low consensus as to the nature of the goals, and this too is important information for the process audit since lack of consensus suggests difficulty in program implementation with several sets of objectives pursued by different managers.

A second concern is who established the program objectives, and the process by which they were developed. Is a single executive responsible for the specification of goals, and to what extent were others involved in the process? Moreover, the goals need to be assessed in terms of the historical evolution of corporate goals. Have the goals changed since the program was initially established? Have the conditions that originally led to the development of goals and the program changed? How? Such questions are a basic part of the social process audit procedure.

A related aspect of goal analysis focuses on the internal or external nature of goal development. External pressures in the form of social group pressures, public opinion, unfavorable comparisons with other firms in the industry, union demands, governmental regulations, or judicial action may have the effect of imposing programmatic objectives upon the company. Conversely, internal goals may evolve from worker discontent, significant changes in such factors as costs, resources, and productivity, or perhaps the zeal of certain company executives. In the safety area, for example, a corporation may find that its safety record is far below industry norms. Or it may perceive that provisions of the OSHA will necessitate certain actions. Internal pressures may be noted in the increase in accident frequency rates, worker unrest over unsafe working conditions, or the desire of a key executive to provide an accident-free environment for employees. Such distinctions will be useful in determining the effectiveness of various programs. For example, a company may respond to external pressures by establishing a program that fails to meet the objectives and concerns of the external groups, or the program may be implemented without the necessary involvement of the external interests. Of course, specific goals can be a mixture of internal and external antecedents, but in any case the internal and/or external nature of goals must be assessed.

A corollary point concerns the existence of noncompany goals with respect to the specific program. For instance, several major firms have "adopted" inner-city high schools. The social auditor needs to know whether or not management is aware of the objectives of the high school's faculty, administration, parents, and students. Are these noncompany goals accounted for in the various high school adoption programs? Or is the program merely serving some needs of the corporation? In the same vein, the auditing process needs to account for employee goals as distinct from corporate goals. The commitment of some managers and workers to such a high school program may stem from a different set of objectives from those of the corporation. Does the program accommodate the employees' goals? In any case, the social process audit technique should examine the existence and nature of noncompany goals as well as employee goals. The social nature of the programs being audited almost by definition implies that there will be interested groups outside the company. The social process audit should carefully assess whether such external or employee interests are or should be involved in the program.

Another step in the analysis of program goals concerns how they are operationalized for program implementation. An important issue here is the nature of the program and its goals. A broad open-ended goal such as the improvement of the neighborhood in which the factory operates cannot be effectively implemented or measured without the establishment of some kind of operational goals and programs—for example, the commitment to hire 70 percent of new workers from within the neighborhood. This can be contrasted with a program and goal that is already operational in character—raising $5 million from within the corporate community to build a new wing for a hospital. In this latter case, of course, further goal operationalization could be helpful for the implementation of the fund-raising campaign. The social process audit should gather information about the operationalization of goals and the assignment of responsibility for the various goals. By analyzing operational goals one can ask questions about the substance of the goals as well as the process of goal setting. Inconsistencies and contradictions may appear between goals established at one level of management and those developed in another part of the organization for the same program or for a different function. Indeed, the mapping of operational goals as understood throughout the organization in a means-end analysis fashion may help to uncover problems or to suggest areas for improvement. Similarly, the establishment of goals without the participation of those who have the responsibility for achieving them not only may frustrate the responsible manager but also may contribute to an unsuccessful social effort by the company.

Inputs to the Program

For a knowledgeable assessment of a corporate social program, it is important to obtain accurate data about the inputs and resources committed to the effort. Such information can be analyzed in relation to program goals and achievements to determine whether the particular activity should be continued, modified, or stopped. To provide a sound basis for such an assessment, comprehensive input data are needed. Furthermore, a careful analysis of program inputs may reveal inadequate or inappropriate resources to achieve the objectives. More effective allocation of resources may result in a more successful program. In short, comprehensive information about program inputs is necessary for the creative management of corporate social programs.

Important as such information is, it is also difficult to obtain in a comprehensive, accurate, and timely fashion. The many problems involved have too often dissuaded managers from attempting to obtain input information. In some instances, the costs are deemed to be too small to warrant extensive concern and assessment; in others, the program is thought to have great social value regardless of the cost; or sometimes external pressures require the implementation of the program and the associated inputs. There are many reasons why management may not wish to gather input data for a cost-benefit analysis, but the lack of such data may hinder the development of a more effective and better organized program.

The social process audit methodology calls for the identification, data collection, and analysis of four types of costs or inputs to corporate social programs. Company inputs are the most obvious type, but the specific nature of company costs may vary from program to program. Dollar outlays by the company, the contribution of material resources, and amounts of employee time required by the program are all company inputs to the program or costs incurred by the company in support of the effort. Similarly, some programs should be allocated a share of overhead expenses incurred by the company. Ideally, all of these inputs can be translated into precise dollar figures so that the total corporate input can be tabulated. However, it is also important to maintain disaggregated cost figures since efforts to improve program management should be based on a careful analysis of the nature of corporate commitment in relation to program objectives. It is important to note that we are not just referring to a need to increase corporate commitments. Far more important is the ability to determine the appropriateness of the resource mix given the program objectives. Contributions of significant funds to minority community organizations may be less effective than assigning sensitive and proficient employees to aid in job training of minority workers. Similarly, a safety program may achieve the greatest success by concentrating on the personal contacts necessary to establish safety consciousness among employees rather than on advertising campaigns, new equipment, and so on. Comprehensive corporate input figures (even if not precisely accurate) are crucial for a social process audit.

Another benefit of analyzing corporate inputs is the ability to assess resource utilization at different levels of responsibility. The various types of costs of any particular program may be inefficiently and unevenly distributed over the organization. A given program may require extensive employee and managerial involvement at some levels, much less at other levels or parts of the organization. Moreover, analysis of the corporate inputs for several programs may indicate that certain parts of the organization are perhaps too heavily involved in social programs given their other responsibilities while other areas are not at all involved and should be.

Obtaining corporate cost information is not an easy task. Often the costs are absorbed or hidden in other functions and thus not readily available. In such cases, estimates of inputs may provide reasonable approximations of program costs. Of particular importance are salary figures, direct financial outlays, and dollar equivalents of materials used in the program. Often the social auditor will find that many corporate personnel have little information about the cost of a program, their particular inputs, or how even to conceptualize accounting for inputs. Consequently, the social analyst needs to be able to ask the right kinds of questions to get the information needed from various parts of the firm. In some cases, input data are available in diverse places but have not been collected and codified; this the auditor may have to initiate. Finally, in many areas, the necessary information may not be available; in this situation, the best the auditor can do is to suggest that for the purposes of future social process audits the company would do well to generate appropriate data and then to indicate the types of data needed.

A final type of corporate cost that ideally should be included in the social process audit is that of opportunity costs. While it is unlikely that this can be quantified for many programs or even estimated for others, it is an important concept that should in some fashion be incorporated in the social process audit. Accounting for it in the input or cost part of the audit may be one strategy; another may be to consider opportunity costs when assessing achievements of the program; in other situations, it may be considered in the overall evaluation of the program and its implementation. Regardless of how it is done, the consideration of opportunity costs is crucial to the evaluation of a corporate social program.

Examination of the composition and distribution of company resources can alert the analyst to possible problems or to areas in need of more intense monitoring. For example, the actual time spent by managers may be far more (or much less) than intended by top management and may differ from record data. Patterns may emerge indicating that too much managerial time may be involved or that resources committed resemble the "lobbing money over the ghetto wall" approach. Technical as opposed to managerial assistance may be a better way to support community development programs. Regardless of the specifics, the social process audit should enable a corporation to assess its own commitments to social programs with the objectives of (1) improving program management, and (2) encouraging some form of cost-benefit analysis.

Another type of input to corporate social program is provided by the employees of the firm. Employee inputs are resources contributed by the employee and without compensation by the company. If the company does compensate the employee (for example, social program work may be performed on company time), then such inputs would be picked up in the calculation of company inputs. There are many programs that depend upon the willingness of salaried and nonsalaried employees to give their time to the effort. There are direct costs associated with these activities such as transportation and equipment costs as well as opportunity costs regarding alternative ways of using one's time. The harried executive or the hourly worker trying to make ends meet may find that voluntary participation in a corporate-sponsored social program takes time away from relaxing pursuits, getting to know one's children better, or fixing up the house. The basic point is that a true assessment of the inputs to a program must take into account the direct and indirect costs incurred by employees. Many a program is in essence subsidized by employees without the full recognition of such inputs or any reward by the company. However, an attempt to estimate these inputs may indicate that the program is too expensive from the employee's point of view, that it needs more official corporate support in the form of resources, or that it is creating much ill will among those needed to implement the program.

The social process audit also attempts to assess the nature and extent of noncompany inputs to a particular corporate social program. Too often the costs of social projects are assessed only from the corporate point of view while the actual and, by implication, needed commitments of others not associated with the company are not considered. In adopting a high school, the company program actually depends heavily upon the resource inputs of the school's faculty, administration, and students. A community development and improvement program requires the commitment of resources by a wide variety of formal and informal community groups. The fundamental point is that often by definition company social programs have a large noncompany component whose direct, indirect, and opportunity costs should be assessed. Consequently, it is important for the social process audit to generate information about the non-company groups making resource inputs to the program. Such an analysis helps management to realize that the program is not solely a corporate program and that incurred costs are more than just corporate costs.

This aspect of the social process audit allows for a more complete cost-benefit analysis of such programs. It also forces recognition of the resource commitments of the noncompany groups and allows questions to be asked about whether the noncompany groups—often the beneficiaries—are obtaining enough benefit from the programs, given their costs. From the perspective of program management, assessments can be undertaken regarding the nature and amount of noncompany costs. Would a different mix of company and noncompany inputs improve the program? Can these outside groups afford the costs they are incurring? Does the company program require more noncompany resources than is necessary? Given the inputs of noncompany groups, are they effectively involved in the goal-setting and planning phases of management? Is their counsel and participation solicited in the implementation of the program? Are they given enough credit for their contributions to the effort? In essence, the step of identifying and assessing resource inputs from noncompany groups emphasizes the fact that often these programs are not just company programs. The non-company aspect needs to be recognized and incorporated for effective program management.

There is another kind of input, or, more accurately, cost, which ought to be considered—the concept of social costs incurred in the process of pursuing social programs. In many cases, these costs may be difficult to identify, hard to measure, and not very important. However, the general concept of social costs is as appropriate for a social program as it is for the normal functions of doing business. For example, company participation in community improvement efforts might involve the use of company trucks and other equipment. The consumption of gas and the resulting vehicle pollution are as much social costs as if these vehicles were transporting products from factory to market. Admittedly, this is a rather minor point, but social costs should be considered where possible.

The social process audit methodology seeks to identify, evaluate, and analyze the various inputs to or costs of a particular social program. The four types of inputs discussed above argue forcefully that corporate social projects frequently involve resource commitments by employees, noncompany groups, and society that are not often incorporated in the usual assessment of program costs. If all four types of inputs are considered, a more comprehensive cost-benefit analysis can be undertaken. Moreover, a careful analysis of the amount and nature of resource inputs in the light of program goals and implementation may reveal ways in which input adjustments may improve the program. The difficulties of accurately measuring many of these costs are obvious, but the procedure suggested should greatly enhance the ability to ask crucial questions about a social program and its implementation.

Implementation of the Program

A critical aspect of the social process audit approach is the attempt to obtain information and generally assess how the particular social program is implemented. It is this element of the technique that makes it different from other social accounting efforts, which tend to look at aggregate data in pursuit of a bottom-line figure. Thus, the data collected should provide information about how the program is implemented—allowing eventually an evaluation of the strengths and weaknesses of program implementation. Having this information greatly aids efforts to improve the operations of the program, and as such the implementation assessment should be considered as a useful tool for managers.

Data need to be gathered about the official and unofficial structure and dynamics of the social program. The lines of authority and the patterns of responsibility for the various program components should be clearly identified, taking care to note the extent to which people outside of the company have important management functions. A thorough analysis should be conducted, for it may be found that a relatively minor part of the structure drastically reduces the effectiveness of the program. Numerous firms have found, for example, that their affirmative action efforts were being obstructed by hostile receptionists. In the safety program we analyzed, workers failed to take the program seriously when immediate supervisors seemed to disregard safety practices. In a similar fashion, the nature and dynamics of the program procedures need to be analyzed since they may contribute to or detract from the success of the effort. The actions undertaken and the routine processes followed often have an important effect on the success of a program. For example, a contributions-in-kind program may be consistently undermined by procedures in the warehouse that dispose of damaged goods through the program.

Another aspect of program implementation is the communication and feedback system associated with the effort. The communication of program objectives and top management commitment to the program throughout the organization is a critical component in the success of any program. Far too often, the statements on top management interest and support are perceived to be rather perfunctory expressions with little real meaning for or acceptance by lower-level personnel. Where this is the case, the implementation of the program will suffer.

In addition to investigating the communication of managerial commitment and program goals, the social process audit procedure calls for an examination of feedback mechanisms regarding program implementation. Of concern is information about how the social program is operating at various parts of the process. In the area of affirmative action efforts, feedback should be obtained about the recruitment process, the hiring process, the training process, the counseling process, and other aspects. Bottom-line feedback revealing the number of minority employees hired will not allow a full assessment of how the program is being implemented and may mask problems in the implementation procedure. In the safety program studied, the feedback system regarding implementation was sometimes good and at other times nonexistent. Moreover, there was at times a difference between what was supposed to have been built into the structure and process and what actually transpired. For example, meetings that should have been held to discuss safety matters with workers sometimes were not. In sum, a feedback system focusing on the implementation of the program, not just the outcome, is a critical part of the social process audit.

Of course, there does need to be feedback regarding the results or benefits of the program. This represents the bottom line, and executives need no introduction to the concept. However, its application to social programs is often not undertaken, with managers failing to establish a comprehensive system to provide the necessary feedback. Moreover, information is needed on more than just the corporate view of the program results. Consequently, there needs to be an effort to determine whether the corporation obtains feedback from extra-company interests. The contributions-in-kind program suffered from the fact that no systematic effort was made to find out the reactions of the recipients of the goods. Thus, management had no idea whether the program was being effectively implemented from the beneficiaries' point of view. Nor did they have information regarding the benefits received. Thus, damaged and inappropriate merchandise was being delivered without management knowledge. From the corporate perspective, all was going well. From the recipient's point of view, much could easily have been improved. The social process audit is designed to focus attention on and uncover problems in the communications and feedback systems.

The previous discussion emphasizes again the necessity of gathering information from interests and beneficiaries outside of the corporation. By definition, a corporate social program involves groups beyond the ranks of management, and thus communication and feedback systems ought to include these extracompany groups. Whether they do or not is something that the social process audit must find out by obtaining information about the external flow of communication as well as the internal communications about the program. Does top management initiate the program with or without the participation of external groups or lower-level personnel—communication at this stage flowing from top down with little information going in the reverse direction? Similarly, is there any information flow regarding how the program is being implemented? Does that which exists go back to top management at some point? If so, are those who are responsible for the corporate activity also in the position of reporting to top management how it is going? Would those responsible be likely to indicate that they are doing an unsatisfactory job? The point is that communications and feedback mechanisms need to be assessed from the point of view of the flow and direction of the communication.

Obtaining information about the existence and nature of control mechanisms is another basic part of the social process audit technique. Are there formal or informal procedures established to alert management to problems in the program, or does a program once started seem to continue without much managerial control? As mentioned, the internal or external location of these control points and mechanisms should be noted by the process audit. Also, whether the control mechanisms are activated routinely or only in response to a request from management may be useful to know.

A final aspect of the implementation part of the process audit focuses on information about the personnel involved in implementing the program. Generally, matters such as the selection of the personnel, their qualifications, the training offered, and the reward structure for effective management should be assessed by the social process audit. Particularly in the social program area, there are many examples of companies selecting critical personnel who have neither the interest, the skill, nor the commitment to be effective. Other managers may have the interest and commitment but not the requisite abilities to deal with community organizations, for example. Whether the company aids such an employee by helping to prepare him for his tasks is an important piece of information for the process audit.

Similarly, it is useful to gather data on the nature of the reward system under which the manager or hourly worker works. If the manager, for example, has other tasks, such as production quotas or sales goals, it is necessary to find out whether and in what way he or she is rewarded for doing a good job on the social program. In evaluating the manager's performance, is any importance ascribed to his or her efforts on behalf of the social program relative to other duties? If personal success depends solely on performance in areas other than the social program, then there is no reason for managers or employees to pay much attention to the program. For example, if line personnel in production feel that they are rewarded solely on the basis of their ability to produce, then they are not likely to make major efforts on behalf of a safety program, feeling that there is no personal payoff in doing more than is minimally necessary. This same effort should be undertaken for people outside of the company who have a role in program implementation. Is a teacher or administrator rewarded for working with a company in a program designed to keep children in school, or do their efforts count for naught during the annual review? Even though the company may not have any direct control over such a situation, knowledge of the problem and subsequent action may enable the firm to improve the program's implementation.

To conclude our explanation of the implementation section of the social process audit, it should be stressed again that a crucial objective of this technique is the evaluation of the process by which social programs are managed. This requires obtaining information about the management of the program. In turn, this step enables managers to improve the nature and implementation of the corporate social program.

Outputs of the Program

The social process audit also attempts to gather information on the outputs of particular social programs. For other types of social auditing procedures the output data may be the only important information, but the social process audit technique recognizes program results as being only one part of a broader effort to assess the effectiveness and management of a corporate social program. Output data are collected because they can be compared with the objectives established by management and with the inputs to the program. In addition, the nature of the program results may give some clues as to problems in the implementation of the program. Thus, the analysis of program results is important by itself, and in conjunction with other information obtained is useful for a more precise assessment of a corporate social program.

The measurement of program output will of course vary with the nature of the program. However, it must be stressed that nonfinancial measures of program results may often be more useful and accurate than financial measures. Also, in developing mechanisms for obtaining information about outputs, qualitative indicators may have more meaning than quantitative measures that are artificial and contrived. Indeed, carefully developed and consistently applied efforts at collecting qualitative data may generate the kind of information necessary for the social process audit technique.

Outputs can be thought of as the end products of a program resulting from actions taken in the operation of that program. As such there are two broad categories of outputs for which information should be obtained—on the one hand, there are the positive results or benefits of a particular program, but on the other hand, there may exist negative outputs on which information should be obtained and analyzed. Managers of social programs sometimes seek information about the positive results of their efforts, but rarely do they concern themselves with the negative outcomes, assuming instead that good intentions do not produce negative results. However, a conscious attempt to identify and gather data on the negative aspects of a corporate social program will enable management to change the program to reduce the negative results or perhaps even to decide to eliminate the program.

A well-meaning effort to provide employment for "hard-core unemployables" may also have the effects of disrupting production, causing envy among those workers not hired under such a program, and overburdening first-line supervisors who now have complex training and personnel problems in addition to the usual difficulties of fulfilling production goals. Similarly, a special program designed to introduce un- or underemployed women liberal arts graduates to the intricacies of the business world, to prepare them for jobs with corporations, may have the unintended but unfortunate effect of raising expectations beyond the capacity to meet them. Thus, one result of such a program might be the existence of partially prepared but very alienated women unable to find a job commensurate with their skill level and self-images. The general point, and it is a crucial one, is that information about the positive and the negative outputs of the program should be obtained.

On this point, though, it is important to consider secondary or tertiary program outputs that affect society in a positive and/or a negative fashion. In other words, a program designed to have a definite impact on a particular target group may have positive or negative effects for other parts of society too. These second- and third-order social costs and social benefits ought to be considered in the overall assessment even though reliable information may be difficult to obtain. A corporate program to use its own personnel and craftsmen to aid in the renovation of a community facility may have the undesirable effect of taking business away and thus making less viable small contracting businesses located in the community.

In gathering data about program outputs, the analyst needs to identify the specific nature of the outputs, keeping in mind both the qualitative and quantitative dimensions of results and the negative and positive dimensions. Care should be taken to look beyond the often limited and self-serving results that program managers may grasp as evidence of an effective program. For example, in the safety program audited, an accident frequency rate was relied upon to measure part of the program output. The problem was that the managers had not developed an accident severity measure that provided data on the severity of the occurring accidents. The failure to examine creatively the nature of program outputs had prevented management from getting a different (and less desirable) picture of the program results. Frequently, it is the social process auditor who can bring in the fresh perspective and the searching inquiry necessary for analysis of program results.

The social process audit technique also calls for the collection of information about the recipients of the outputs of the social program. The intended targets vary with the specific program, but it is also important to identify unintended recipients of program outputs. Thorough investigation may reveal that a corporate community action program has the unexpected effect of strengthening (or weakening) indigenous community organizations. Thus, the failure to identify those who are affected by the program (receive the outputs) will result in an incomplete assessment of the program results. In addition, analysis of the recipients may uncover patterns and characteristics not readily observable as a result of a superficial examination. A corporate college scholarship program for children of employees may be consistently awarded to the offspring of managerial personnel as opposed to those of workers. Yet the program intent may have been to make a college education more available to the families of workers—not managers.

In analyzing the recipients of program outputs, it is also useful to consider the intra—or extra—company nature of the recipients. Programs designed to provide corporate support for things like Junior Achievement also affect the firm's managers who become involved. Depending upon a host of variables, the executives may or may not benefit from their attempts to help. Such an experience may provide needed diversion from the demands of the firm, and it may also expose the executive to new perspectives not found in the closed corporate world. For others, though, such an experience might be considered only a bother. A safety program will benefit the workers, but it may also have the results of reducing lost production time as well as insurance costs. In such a case, there are a number of different program results.

In short, the analysis of outputs must dig deeper than the obvious and intended results. The social process audit must seek information on unintended outcomes, which may be either positive or negative or both in impact. The careful scrutiny and assessment of program outputs will aid in general program evaluation as well as in the improvement of program operation.

Analysis of Program Processes

Having completed the data collection and analysis for the elements of a corporate social program as discussed above, the next step in the social process audit procedure is a general evaluation of the program. More specifically, the overall analysis of the program seeks to examine the relationships among the factors as they interact in the operation of the program. In other words, this final step of the procedure assesses how well and how the various parts of the program fit together to fulfill the objectives initially established by management.

Beginning with goals, it is useful to obtain information on the consistency of program goals. As noted earlier, a single program may have several different and perhaps even somewhat contradictory goals as understood by various managers and employees. Moreover, external groups may have their own objectives for the corporate program in which they are participating. Recognizing the likelihood of several different goals, the corporate goal or set of goals establishes a benchmark by which the program can be evaluated.

To simplify matters, let us assume that we are able to identify a specific corporate goal for the social program. Based on information obtained earlier, some interesting analyses and assessments can be made. By comparing outputs to the goal, we receive an immediate, if incomplete, reading as to whether the program objectives were achieved. We also have the information to compare the goals as defined with the unintended positive and negative results of the program. These bottom-line-type figures will provide the basis for an overall judgment of the success or failure of the program. However, since the social process audit technique is also designed to evaluate, and thus help improve, the management of social programs, our analysis does not end with a comparison of goals and outcomes.

The goal defined can also be compared with the inputs made available for the particular program. It may be felt that there are insufficient resources committed to the effort, but equally as likely will be the realization that the mix of inputs is inappropriate. For example, an effort to convince teen-agers to stay in school may suffer not from the lack of corporate resources but instead from the failure to obtain the help of those with whom the students are readily able to identify. In another instance, financial resources may be a less effective input than technical assistance and cooperation by corporate personnel. This analysis may be facilitated by undertaking a two-step comparison that looks at the resources committed in light of the program results that may reveal problems in the area of program inputs.

Similarly, given the goal, another important question is whether the implementation of the program has contributed to the achievement of objectives or not. More important is the attempt to determine whether and how program implementation can be improved to enhance the achievement of the objectives established by management. Again, a careful analysis of program results may provide clues regarding problems in the implementation of the program. For example, some unexpected negative feedback from certain recipients of the program outputs should alert the analyst to the possibility of difficulties in the implementation of the program in this sector.

Finally, the program results can be assessed in the light of the background of the program. There may exist definite incongruence between the root causes of the program and the achievements of the program.

This analysis of a management goal for a social program can, of course, be conducted for the multiple goals more characteristic of company social programs. While a more complex process, the objectives of such an analysis are basically the same—to assess the elements and procedures that are supposed to contribute to the achievement of the goals.

The existence of multiple program goals also requires the analyst to determine whether there are conflicts among the different goals and their implementation procedures. Does the method of achieving one goal adversely or positively affect the pursuit of another goal? Phrased another way, are individual goals consistent with one another and to what extent are the processes of achieving these goals supportive or in conflict? In the safety program reviewed, the attempt to stimulate safety consciousness among workers could well lead to the reporting of more rather minor accidents. This development would very much conflict with the objective of reducing the accident frequency rate for a particular plant. Thus, horizontal inconsistencies among goals and their implementation procedures may occur.

Another form of inconsistency may be that which exists between a corporate social program and other nonsocial corporate goals. Thus, conflicts between the pursuit of (1) profit, production, sales, and so on, and (2) social programs often confront managers. Such conflicts do not necessarily have to be resolved— the competing objectives and procedures may be allowed to coexist. However, it will be important for the improvement of program management to be aware of these broader conflicts and inconsistencies.

CONCLUSIONS

The analysis of process step in the social process audit procedure is designed to examine the linkages among the various elements of a particular program. In addition, it seeks to investigate the relationship between one corporate objective and its implementation efforts and other corporate goals of a social or nonsocial nature. This step, in conjunction with the earlier parts of the social process audit methodology, will enable management to scrutinize closely their social programs from the perspective of improving the programs as well as generally evaluating them.

However, we have presented a framework to be adapted to particular situations, not a blueprint for all to follow. The specifics of corporations, personnel, and programs may require adaptations in the framework, but it can serve as a strategy for action by executives who seek to evaluate their corporation's social programs.

4

CONDUCTING A SOCIAL PROCESS AUDIT

As discussed in previous chapters, the social process audit can provide information useful to managers in their efforts to improve the management of social programs. However, in a particular situation, the audit can be no more effective or useful than the way in which it is implemented by those conducting the audit. The difficult task of implementing a social process audit is made even more complex by the attitudinal, organizational, and political problems discussed in Chapter 2. In this chapter, we build upon some of the issues raised earlier to focus more specifically on how the auditor can obtain the information necessary for the audit. The social auditor needs skills and imagination not only to collect and analyze the data but also to overcome the serious concerns examined earlier. We begin this chapter by developing some of the strategic considerations important for the success of the audit and then turn to a more technical discussion of how the needed information can be obtained. It should be noted that skills in both the strategic and the technical areas are mandatory for an effective auditor.

STRATEGIC CONSIDERATIONS FOR THE AUDITOR

Most organizations, be they public or private, are reluctant to endorse enthusiastically a close examination of the processes, procedures, and general management of their social programs. This hesitancy by no means implies that the organization has things to hide from the auditors. More likely it is the understandable dislike by managers at all levels of having outsiders poke around in their own business with the possibility that some weaknesses in current management will be found and with all suggestions made implying some degree of criticism of existing managers. The sensitivity of program administrators is natural and ought not be dismissed or ignored by the auditing team. Moreover, the problem is heightened by the newness of social auditing and the fact that most managers are unfamiliar with the approach and its objectives.

To overcome this reluctance, telling arguments can be presented to managers by the auditor that show how the social process audit can help in such areas as achievement of program objectives, improvement of company image, and cost control. In addition, the auditor should explain to the managers involved the nature of the process audit as well as its objectives, for these people are in a position to facilitate or retard severely the effort to conduct an audit. To further the understanding and participation of these managers in the audit, a useful strategy with substantive and procedural payoff is to ask for their advice, obtain information from them, and generally discuss approaches and problems associated with the audit procedure. Such efforts may not only help in the implementation of the audit but may also increase the acceptance and reduce the suspicions of these people. While the auditor cannot agree to report only the positives and skirt the negatives, it is important to stress the auxiliary and supportive nature of the technique and to assure the relevant managers that the auditors will aid them in interpreting the results and recommendations. Those responsible for the program should not feel that the audit merely seeks to check up on them or that the results will be reported to top management without any discussion with those most directly involved. There are many steps that can be taken to obtain the cooperation of the involved managers, but in spite of all such efforts the concerns and fears may continue to exist. In this case, the auditor will have to proceed with particular care while constantly stressing the supportive contributions of the audit.

One of the strategic problems that the auditor may encounter is the existence of a social program that cuts across several functional lines. Thus, while the personnel people may be exceptionally open to the auditing of a safety program, the manufacturing division may see the efforts as likely to interrupt production and perhaps to question lines of authority. In this same example, the labor relations people may be concerned about relations with the union, and the legal staff may be worried about all manner of things relating to secrecy, the possibility of law suits, government interference, and many other such legal matters. The social auditor will have to be skilled both in identifying these potential barriers before they become insurmountable and in trying to alleviate the concerns.

Moreover, the social auditing team may have to act as a mediator or facilitator between different departments to obtain the approval and cooperation of those involved. Sometimes organizational jealousy and politics will contribute to the conflict, but in other cases what is thought to be beneficial to one unit of the organization will be perceived as being threatening to the interests of a different unit. The auditor needs to be sensitive to these problems, try to understand the causes, and then take appropriate remedial steps. Where the intraorganizational conflicts are particularly severe, the auditing team may find it necessary to engage in a kind of shuttle diplomacy to obtain the necessary approvals.

One difficulty faced by the social auditor is the identification of the nature and location of useful information existing within the corporation. Few organizations, public or private, will have structured their information to be responsive to the needs of a social auditing team. Consequently, data sets are often incomplete, inappropriately organized and classified for the social audit, dispersed and hidden among different functional units, or absent. Once relevant information is found, the auditors may have to rework the data to conform to the needs of the social audit. Our experience has shown also that it is often necessary for the social auditor to dig into the files or old record books in order to obtain the information needed. A passive, armchair approach relying on crisp computer printouts is rarely feasible.

A similar and potentially more severe problem (especially, but by no means exclusively) for outside auditors is the question of secrecy. Whether it is fear of external disclosure or concern that others inside the corporation will use the information to damage a person's career, information sources may be rigidly closed off to the auditing team. This issue is no doubt exacerbated by a widespread sense of antagonism that seems to exist among business managers and parts of the society. There are no easy techniques for overcoming these suspicions except in the careful and sensitive attempt to indicate the relevance of the work and in the professional conduct of the auditing team itself, as will be discussed shortly. Even if the best information source is blocked, alternate means of getting the same material from different sources may be found.

The problems mentioned above and in Chapter 2 will tax the patience and creativity of social auditors. However, the auditors must remember that while they may be familiar with and committed to the social process audit it will be unfamiliar, for a while at least, and probably threatening to many managers. Therefore, it is desirable that the auditors seek to explain with some degree of precision how the social process audit can contribute to effective management. It may be useful to provide examples of social audits that have actually been conducted in order to show how they have aided management. Secondly, relevant managers should be asked to participate in the planning of the audit procedure itself so that they feel it is something they are involved in, not something being done to them. Finally, the auditors should try to identify the source of the concerns of managers who create obstacles and alleviate their fears where possible.

The question of internal versus external auditors has important ramifications for the conduct of the audit. Internal auditors have some significant advantages. They are, of course, familiar with the company, its personnel, and its procedures, and time and effort will not be lost in the orientation process. Moreover, company auditors will not confront the same degree of concern about secrecy of corporate information that external auditors might face. Internal auditors will be viewed as coworkers who understand the corporation and not as outsiders from whom the manager must protect the company. In addition, since internal auditors will continue with the company, they will be more readily available to help in the revision and adjustment of the program in response to the audit's recommendations. A further advantage is that relying upon internal social auditors may result in the establishment of a cadre of managers effective in evaluating social programs. Probably the out-of-pocket cost of an audit conducted by company personnel will be less than that incurred by relying upon external auditors.

However, there are serious disadvantages associated with internal auditors, many of which represent the reverse side of the advantages just discussed. The familiarity of internal auditors with the company may prevent a fresh and more objective look at the program. Company loyalty and personal friendships, as well as company politics, may result in the biasing of analysis, which would not be present among external auditors. A willingness to give the benefit of the doubt can retard the critical analysis so crucial to a social process audit. Moreover, as discussed in Chapter 2, external auditors may be more likely to obtain honest opinions and full information than internal auditors. Subordinates may fear that their honesty will harm their careers, and noncompany groups may be concerned that the company will consider them ingrates if they identify weaknesses in the management of the program and perhaps even end the program as a result. In addition, the proper use of external auditors would ensure that their counsel would be sought for the revision and improvement of the program. Therefore, it is important that the external auditing group develop mechanisms to facilitate this process. Finally, the skills of the external auditor may also mean that the company is obtaining better information in less time than if company personnel were used. In this way, using external auditors may be cost effective.

While we tend to feel that companies will be best served initially by using external auditors, there is no doubt that developing company personnel to perform audits will be valuable and necessary because of the lack of skilled external auditors. Of course, the nature of the program and the company as well as the availability of social auditors inside and outside the company will affect the decision of how the audit should be conducted. Depending upon the size and importance of the program, a company might wish to have external auditors involved every four or five years with internal audits conducted in the interim.

Whether the audit is conducted by internal or external personnel, it is crucial that the auditors proceed in a professional manner, for it is in this fashion that credibility will be established and maintained. They need to be able to respect confidences and understand the sensitivities and anxieties that are bound to be present. They should be skilled in overcoming the concerns and obstacles with which their efforts are likely to be greeted. Moreover, their abilities and attitudes as professionals should be beyond question and should inspire confidence among company and noncompany personnel. Finally, where the audit itself is to be an internal document for company management, it is important that the auditors not reveal the results to outsiders. A few misplaced remarks, accidentally or not, may cause company officials to shy away from future audits that they fear might be used to embarrass the company or its people. We cannot stress enough the need for professionalism among the auditors, whether internal or external, for it is through professional conduct, and of course useful results, that social auditing will gain greater acceptance.

In addition to the creation of confidence and credibility, there are several other strategic considerations for the auditor to be aware of. One involves the need to provide management at all levels with feedback on the results of the audit. The final audit report is not sufficient. The auditor ought not to collect information from and rely upon the cooperation of managers and others without taking the time later on to discuss with them the findings of the audit related to their particular areas of concern. Without this direct feedback, these managers will not have benefited from the audit, will be anxious about the results, may feel merely used by the auditors, and will be reluctant to cooperate in the future. As a result, the auditor should ensure that meaningful feedback is provided that represents more than a cursory reporting of results. In doing this, the auditor may have increased the receptivity of such people to attempts to improve the management of the social program.

As discussed in Chapter 1, a number of different goals are associated with the various types of social audits that have been proposed. We have noted, too, in Chapter 3, that there are several different analyses involved and purposes served by the social process audit. Top management may want to use a social process audit to determine whether a program should be continued in the light of its costs and its accomplishments. Or perhaps the purpose may be to evaluate how the program is managed and to identify ways to improve its effectiveness. It is possible that the goals and objectives of the program should be revised to reflect more adequately the capabilities of the company and the interests and concerns of the beneficiaries of the program. The point is that there may be a number of different reasons why management wants to undertake a social process audit. Consequently, the auditors will want to discuss these alternatives and others with management, indicating how the audit's results can be used for various purposes.

Another issue to be considered by the social auditor is the question of the time and cost of each audit. Naturally, these will vary with the size and complexity of the program, the number and types of noncompany groups involved, the openness of the corporation to social auditing, and management's objectives for the audit. Thus, while a rule-of-thumb mechanism for determining time and cost is not available, it should be understood that a thorough audit and analysis are expensive. Probably it is unnecessary for most social programs to be audited every year, thereby reducing the overall amounts spent for social auditing.

However, periodic auditing is important in order to monitor and evaluate the effectiveness and activities of that effort. In any event, the auditor should discuss with management the probable cost of the audit and the amount of time needed to complete it.

Thus far in this chapter we have discussed some major strategic issues confronting the social auditor. While we have indicated various strategies that may be useful to consider, the precise implementation strategy will depend upon the nature of the program, the degree of management commitment and support, management's objectives, and the skills of the auditors. Although the implementation strategy will therefore vary with the circumstances, the auditors must be certain to think consciously about such a strategy and to develop and implement one with considerable care.

TECHNIQUES FOR OBTAINING INFORMATION

Information of various types is needed for a social process audit. The auditor will have to be creative and skillful in identifying the types of information needed, finding sources for this information, and then obtaining it. These three steps are critical for a social process audit. In Chapter 3 we examined the types of information needed, and this section of the chapter discusses several techniques to obtain information.

To begin, a distinction between data generation and data collection should be made. Data generation involves the development of information where none currently exists. Obviously, generating data can only follow the determination that the social process audit of a particular program needs certain types of new information for evaluation and assessment. This process of conceptualizing information needs demands practical creativity on the part of the auditor. For example, for many social programs such as the philanthropic contributions program illustrated in Chapter 6, there are no easy or obvious measures of program effectiveness, and the auditors will have to develop such measures. This process of data generation, particularly where it involves new conceptualization and innovation, is a very important part of the social process audit procedure and calls for imagination and skill in the auditor.

Data collection, on the other hand, is concerned with the techniques by which existing information is obtained. It refers to the process of gathering the information in a form meaningful and useful for the purposes of the audit. Like data generation, it requires creativity in conceptualization and implementation and also a lot of hard work. Some information may be readily available and appropriately organized for use in the social audit. Other information may be scattered in various parts of the corporation or organized in an inappropriate fashion. Other needed information may not exist at all. In the first case, the auditor is extremely fortunate; in the second, hard work and persistence are required to track down the information or unscramble it from useless categories; in the third case, the auditor needs to make use of some of the specific techniques of data generation and collection to which we now turn our attention.

Documents, memos, records, and files can provide a wealth of material for the social auditor. These sources may reveal data about costs, initial goals of the program, earlier evaluations of company efforts, and so on. Some of the material will be usable as found; some will have to be interpreted or categorized according to the scheme most useful for the audit. In addition, data will be both quantitative and qualitative in form. Some documents will be straightforward company records while others (such as memoranda) may represent largely the personal expressions or observations of individual managers.

In using these company records, it is important to understand that the information found in them has been collected to serve some prior purpose of the company or its individual managers. Thus, their biases and their purposes will already have determined various characteristics of the information that may or may not be consistent with the needs of the social audit. As a result, it may be useful to discover what the biases are as well as the original intent of the record-keeping or memo writing. In both of the audits illustrated in Chapter 6, the auditors found important information already collected by the company that was useful in the audit. However, the audit of the safety program indicated some shortcomings in the quantitative data collected by the company that caused the auditing team to make some suggestions for improvement.

The auditor needs to be particularly wary of accepting at face value qualitative documents, for they may have been written with the purpose of supporting the views of certain managers. Consequently, the auditor should also seek contradictory evidence among company records in order to check the accuracy of the view presented. In addition, it is valuable to conduct interviews with those who might know something about this aspect of the program. The basic point is that the auditor must investigate—not merely accept. He or she should be alert for and actually seek possibly contradictory evidence, not just information that substantiates the initial version.

Documentary analysis is an important part of the social process audit procedure, but it must be used wisely and sensitively. Furthermore, it requires creativity and dogged investigation to mine the wealth of material likely to be found.

An important technique of data collection is the interview. Managers of the program, their superiors, and subordinates, and program beneficiaries will most likely be interviewed during the audit. In toto, the subject matter of these interviews will cover the full content of the audit (as examined in the previous chapter), although each person interviewed should not be questioned on all aspects of the program. Information desired ranges from factual knowledge about costs, for example, to a description of the development of the program and its goals, to an understanding of the way the program is managed, to assessment of achievements, to attitudes about program objectives and benefits. Consequently, with such a wide variety of information often sought in each interview, the auditor needs to be skilled at extracting factual information, professional assessments, and personal attitudes.

Because of the different types of information desired, many of the interviews will be both structured and unstructured in format. Direct questions will be posed seeking rather specific information, but often the auditor will want to build upon the responses to probe more deeply or to pursue a point raised briefly by the person being interviewed. In addition, unstructured and open questioning is useful when trying to uncover less factual information. The object of this type of questioning is to encourage the person interviewed to discuss the various areas of interest that are central to the social process audit. The auditor's role is to guide the discussion so that the important issues are addressed without imposing a rigid structure on the interview.

Whether structured or nonstructured, the purposes and content of the audit and the organizational role of the person interviewed shape the content of the questions specifically and the interview more generally. Consequently, use of the interview in the social process audit requires extensive planning and knowledge on the part of the auditor. It is not a casual process. Each person or group interviewed can provide information about certain aspects of the corporate social program; questioning on other parts of the program may be futile. Thus, the auditor needs to know rather precisely the type of information to be obtained in each interview, and the interview should be conducted in a fashion to elicit that information. The time and patience of those interviewed are limited, and the auditor will want to maximize the returns from each session.

Some of the interviews will be quite sensitive and will need to be conducted with special care and skill by the auditor. For example, subordinates may be reluctant to criticize the objectives of the program or its management. Interviews with noncompany people who benefit from the corporate program may involve persons of vastly different backgrounds and cultures who are not responsible and may indeed be alienated by the questions and manner that were appropriate for corporate officials. In addition, the beneficiaries of the corporate action may not wish to criticize a program that has produced some positive results even though adjustments might increase the benefits. The task of the auditor is to develop an interviewing style and questions that elicit the information needed. What is effective in one situation is not necessarily effective in others. In some cases, special interviewers ought to be selected for their ability to facilitate the flow of information. For example, auditing a corporate program to aid Mexican-American businesses in southern California may require language and cultural skills not often found among social auditors from a white middle-class background.

The interview technique provides the auditor with the opportunity to cross-check responses from different people in order to piece together a more complete view of the social program. Information obtained in one interview can be compared with the results of other interviews in order to determine accuracy. Gaps in information from one source may be filled in as the result of skilled questioning in other interviews. In addition, interview information should be cross-checked with company records, memos, and other documents and not always taken at face value. In essence, the interview technique, like the others, is an active investigative procedure that the auditor uses to obtain information for the analysis of the corporate social program.

Questionnaires are also a useful technique for certain limited aspects of the social process audit. Since the audit seeks partially to assess the management of a program, the questionnaire is less useful for obtaining in-depth information than other methods described here. Moreover, for the social process audit, it is rarely necessary to get the views of a large number of people where the questionnaire technique is so useful.

However, for some audits, it may be desirable to gather information about a large number of beneficiaries of the program. A company scholarship program sponsored by many company plants in the United States might use a questionnaire to find out how many of the scholarship recipients finished college, majored in what subjects, and continued in graduate school. If the individual plants did not have such information, it might be obtained by a questionnaire. In this case or in some other programs, the auditor might want to probe the attitudes of beneficiaries about the usefulness of the program, its management, their views of the company, or a number of other dimensions. A well-designed questionnaire may be most helpful in some of these cases.

The auditor, though, should recognize the limitations of the questionnaire technique and use it only when appropriate and meaningful. Some people are not familiar with the task of filling out questionnaires, others will see them as a waste of time, and still more will view them as invasions of privacy or snooping mechanisms. Thus, the response rate may be unacceptably low. In addition, information obtained will be limited in scope and depth. Generally, even though it is hard to generalize given the variety of corporate social programs, questionnaires are likely to be most useful when a broad response is needed, probably from beneficiaries of the program, on a rather precise set of dimensions such as factual data and attitudes.

A fourth technique useful in the data-gathering process is that of behavioral observation. Interviews and questionnaires require the conscious response of people to questions about the social program. Behavioral observation, on the other hand, notes and records what is actually occurring, not simply what people think or will say about it. For example, for a program designed to aid minority businesses, the auditor may be able to observe the impact or lack of impact of the technical assistance provided by company personnel. In the safety program audited, we observed that in some departments safety meetings were not being held with the frequency desired by management, indicating that a simple but effective management control system was lacking.

There is no established procedure for conducting behavorial observation as there is with interviews and questionnaires, for efforts of this sort vary with the program, the type of information sought, and the imagination of the social auditor. With the cooperation of managers familiar with the program, the auditor may be able to develop a number of ways to observe behavior that will have a practical payoff for the audit. Overall, it is a useful approach that can provide extensive information without requiring the conscious response of others to questions posed by the auditor. Social auditors should seek to include behavioral observation in their repertoire of techniques.

Some of the information gathered for the audit will be qualitative in nature; other aspects will be quantitative in form. Both quantitative and qualitative kinds of information are necessary for the analysis of corporate social programs, and the four data-gathering techniques discussed above can help secure both types of information. Auditors ought not to shy away from the collection of and reliance upon qualitative information; indeed, they cannot, if they seek to perform the type of analysis discussed in Chapter 3.

In using qualitative information, it is important for the auditor to avoid reliance upon a single source, for then the biases of the source will become those of the audit. Therefore, the auditor should seek information from a number of different sources, consciously attempting to obtain a variety of views. Again, cross-checking of information is a useful technique. Also, the auditor should try to identify the biases of the sources so that the positions expressed are accepted and evaluated in context. In short, qualitative information is a valuable part of the social audit procedure, and sensitive and careful collection of these data and their incorporation into the overall audit are important.

LINKING AUDIT CONTENT AND INFORMATION-GATHERING TECHNIQUES

To conclude this chapter, we need to discuss how the various information-gathering techniques can be used to obtain material useful for each part of the social process audit. Of course, the applicability and utility of each technique varies with the particular program being audited, but an attempt to link the techniques with the content areas of the audit may be useful.

In obtaining information about the *history and general description of the program*, the auditor will rely most heavily on interviews with key corporate personnel and the analysis of documents relating to the program. The interviews can provide much enrichment for the briefer and drier material found in memos and reports and may shed important light on the development of the program. Each technique can be used to expand and question information gathered by the other procedure. The questionnaire technique seems to have little relevance here, but behavioral observation may be useful in analyzing the nature of the program. The data-gathering process will focus primarily on company sources, but valuable information may also be obtained from noncompany sources that may have been instrumental in establishing the program. Information on the history and the nature of the activity will probably be more qualitative than quantitative. To obtain a good picture of the evolution of the program, the auditor may have to engage in careful investigation using several of the techniques discussed.

Information on *program goals* can be garnered through the analysis of documents where company officials have sought to develop objectives for these programs. In other cases, interviewing may be the only way of discovering the goals and objectives of company programs because of the absence of written objectives. However, even where goals are specified in company documents, it is useful to find out during interviews whether these goals are accepted, ignored, or merely camouflage for some other set of goals, which, while not written down, are indeed understood. Interviews may be particularly effective in obtaining information about the goals of individual managers or employees, which sometimes differ from the formal goals of the program. The questionnaire technique may be used to find out the extent to which company goals are known and accepted among company employees, but questionnaires in this instance tend to be of limited usefulness. Again, the information gathered will come primarily from company sources, although creative probing with noncompany people may serve to develop further information regarding the goals of the program. Some programs will have quantitative objectives established, but much of the material in this area will be qualitative in nature.

For information about *program inputs*, document analysis and interviews will again be the most useful techniques. Once the auditor has a good understanding of how the program operated through iterviews with those involved, figures for out-of-pocket costs may be traced and calculations for dollar equivalents of time spent by company personnel can be made. In this part of the audit, accounting records will be important aids to the auditor. Questionnaires will be of limited value since they will be concerned primarily with examining the amount of time spent on the program, but for certain programs direct observation of the activity may provide information about inputs. It is especially important to gather quantitative and qualitative information from noncompany sources, too, for the program may demand significant external inputs.

The auditing of the *program's implementation* will rely upon interviews, behavioral observation, and document analysis. Since the intent of this segment of the audit is to develop material about organizational structure, communication and feedback systems, control mechanisms, and the personnel involved, the auditor has numerous sources from which to gather data. Personnel records and interviews can provide background information on company employees involved in the program. The files for the program will probably reveal part of the organizational structure and communications system, and interviews will elicit further material in these areas. By observing the program in operation, the auditor may be able to identify the patterns of relationship between company personnel and noncompany people involved. Observation of this sort may indicate that the program's organizational structure that has evolved over time differs from that which is thought to exist or was originally planned. As suggested, it is very important that the auditor also obtain information on the implementation of the program from the beneficiaries, for they may well have valuable insights about these matters of which company officials are not aware.

Information about the *outputs of the program*, both positive and negative, can be obtained by use of all four techniques. Documents may contain solid quantitative data about program outputs—the amount and nature of donations, the number of high school students in internship programs, the amount and nature of loans to minority businesses and homeowners, and so forth. In addition, behavioral observation, questionnaires, and interviews may develop information, both quantitative and qualitative, not revealed by the written record. The importance of going beyond the readily available figures should be well understood. The activities performed by the company program may not have the intended effect or may have side effects, and too often the quantitative records measure only activity, not social impact. Here again, the auditor must undertake to obtain information from program beneficiaries and noncompany personnel.

In conclusion, then, this chapter has examined some of the issues and techniques involved in conducting a social process audit. We have discussed this material in general terms, leaving it to the reader to adapt the concepts and ideas expressed to the specific program being audited. Chapter 6 contains summaries of two audits that indicate more precisely the types of information we utilized in those audits, but they are merely illustrative.

The implementation techniques used will vary with the nature of the program, the characteristics of the company and beneficiaries, the obstacles encountered by the auditor, and the skill and creativity of the auditor. At this stage in the development of the social process audit, there are few well-established rules and procedures. Moreover, the most severe limits on such audits are those resulting from a lack of persistence and imagination on the part of the social auditor.

5

REPORTING SOCIAL INFORMATION

Once a social audit has been completed and all of the data have been gathered, the auditors face the additional task of putting the information together in a meaningful and pragmatically useful way. If the audit cannot be brought to the point of producing such a useful social report, it should not be undertaken. The whole purpose of social auditing is to monitor the social performance of organizations so that actions might then be taken to reaffirm or to modify the organization's social policies. An effective report that clearly and concisely sets forth an assessment of social performance can constitute a realistic basis for review of past activities, adjustment of current efforts, and planning for future contingencies.

PRELIMINARY CONSIDERATIONS

The form and content of the social report will be determined in important ways by the audience to which it is addressed. As noted in an earlier chapter, some types of social audits are conducted by outsiders utilizing externally derived data for the purpose of revealing shortcomings in social performance to the general public. These social reports are sometimes inspired by political or ideological factors; hence, their authors are not always careful about completeness of data and methodological rigor since the overriding purpose of the report is to reveal one or more social deficiencies in the organization's performance. In these cases, the intended audience not only cares less about methodological niceties than the purported social impacts but also understands less about such matters. There is little justification for issuing such flawed reports, especially when they are cloaked in the form and language of social auditing or otherwise represented as unbiased and objective accounts.

However, when the audience is internal to the organization and where the purpose of the audit is to provide reliable information to management so that practices and policies can be reviewed, then an entirely different type and content of the social audit can be considered. The social process audit is intended to provide this type of information to management. Completeness of information and proper care in its collection become important, as would be true of any area of concern to management. Decision makers need to command as much relevant information as possible, and they need to know whether the information provided has been reliably and validly compiled and analyzed. Hence, openness and full disclosure should characterize the form and content of a social process audit because the needs of the audience—in this case, the organization's decision makers—dictate such a procedure.

An organization that has undertaken a social process audit may wish in time to communicate the findings to a broader audience, such as shareholders, selected government agencies, or various corporate constituency groups. If so, the data from the audit can be adapted to these uses by selecting those portions of the audit that would be of particular interest to the respective groups, while retaining within the organization that information that is proprietary or of no interest to the general public. The possibility is often present that self-serving vested interests within the organization will withhold some of the audit's findings that are threatening. A combination of an alert corporate constituency, effective legal safeguards, and, especially, managerial integrity can help protect against these practices, which are perhaps inherent in all large-scale organizations. Irrespective of this dilemma, though, the results of a social process audit can be tailored to a variety of uses by an organization's management that wishes to communicate with others both inside and outside the company.

Another decision to be made concerns format. What, after all, should a social audit look like? Should it—can it—emulate a financial audit? Should it contain numbers, or prose, or some combination of the two types of information? And should—can—those numbers be closely related to the numbers in the financial audit? Or, better still, is it possible to combine the data from the social audit with that from the financial audit so that a single integrated audit statement is presented to decision makers?

The answers to these questions will depend upon the type of social audit undertaken. As noted earlier, various attempts have been made to quantify social auditing and to present the information in a form that resembles conventional accounting and financial reporting procedures. Such efforts appear to be not only in the minority but also somewhat less than successful in providing managers with the kind of information needed to assess social impacts. Several commentators have noted that some social impacts are not easily measured while others are not measurable at all in customary ways and many cannot be expressed through numbers alone. There is, moreover, little outward reason for emulating the particular forms of financial reporting, particularly if relevant economic information can be included somewhere in the social audit in a manner that allows managerial judgments to be made about its importance.

This chapter outlines and describes the format for a social process audit, and the next chapter illustrates the form taken by two such audits. Both quantitative and qualitative information are included. Both numbers and prose are employed in the analysis. The audit's form is determined by the nature of the social activity being audited (and therefore by the types and quality of information available) as well as by the audit methodology and the implementation process. All social auditors should remain flexible and pragmatic when considering the report format, remembering at all times that the purpose of the report is to provide information in a useful form to organizational decision makers.

SPECIFIC PURPOSES OF THE SOCIAL REPORT

The social report that results from a social process audit has three specific purposes.

The first is to identify the audit's significant findings. In a sense, this purpose seems almost too obvious and straightforward to merit much explicit consideration, but in the social arena it quickly emerges as the single most important function of the social audit. The reason is simple. Social activities and their accompanying social impacts have not been given the attention that other, more economically oriented operations have received. Not only is less known about these social operations but they customarily rank lower in managerial priorities and receive less time and professional input. Organizational managers often are surprised to learn of the various ways in which their companies affect society. The typical expression is "Why, I never realized we had such an effect upon the community (or our employees, or women in our company, or the local transportation system, and so on)." Therefore, the central purpose of the social report is to present clearly and concisely the major findings of the auditors.

Typically, these findings will include a description of the social activity audited, an identification of the types and numbers of social impacts observed, and enumeration of major accomplishments and problems associated with the social activity, and a set of recommendations. The keynote here at the outset is *identification* of major findings that will be considered of central significance to managerial decision makers. The specific form and sequence in which this information is best presented are discussed below.

The second purpose of the social report is to present detailed information about the findings, together with an analysis of their significance for the organization. A reputable social report to management will be informative and as detailed as is feasible. It will be well documented, it will identify sources of information, and it will be as rigorously analytical in approach and content as is possible, given the type and quality of information available to the auditors. Organizational decision makers should be given a detailed picture of the audited social activity, as well as a description of how those details were developed, so they will command a maximum amount of information to guide their practices and policies in that particular social area.

A third specific purpose of the social report is to indicate social data needs for ongoing and future monitoring of the organization's activities in the audited area. Social auditors often do not find the types and quantities of information needed to identify problems clearly or to provide a firm and reliable basis upon which to develop recommendations. These information gaps do not have to exist forever. One of social auditing's important early contributions is to reveal the existence of these gaps, so that remedial steps may be taken to develop, collect, classify, and make available such data for analytical purposes. So the social report should explicitly indicate what kind of new information is needed and how the data that are already collected may be supplemented or improved in quality to achieve the overall purposes of the social audit.

THE FORM AND CONTENT OF A SOCIAL PROCESS AUDIT

In general, our experience suggests that a social process audit will most usefully contain the following kinds of information arranged in the following format. Each of the outline headings is discussed in some detail below.

A. Introduction
   1. Identification of the audit team
   2. Authorization of the audit
   3. Dates the audit was conducted
B. The Summary Audit Statement
   1. Summary presentation of major findings
   2. Summary statement of recommendations
   3. Reference to details of major findings and recommendations in the body of the report
C. Presentation of Findings
   1. History and rationale of the audited activity
   2. Identification of individual focal areas of the audited activity
      a) Goals
      b) Inputs
      c) Implementation
      d) Outputs
   3. Findings related to each focal area

D. Analysis of Program Processes
   1. Goal achievement
   2. Adequacy of inputs
   3. Effectiveness of implementation
   4. Assessment of outputs
E. Problem Identification and Analysis
   1. With respect to goals
   2. With respect to inputs
   3. With respect to implementation
   4. With respect to outputs
   5. With respect to the data base
      a) Analysis of data needs and accessibility problems
      b) Analysis of existing data collection methods and cost questions
         related to these and alternative methods
F. Recommendations
   1. Recommended actions in each focal area
      a) With respect to goals and goal conflicts
      b) With respect to inputs
      c) With respect to implementation
      d) With respect to outputs
      e) With respect to the data base
G. Audit Evaluation
   1. Limitations of:
      a) The audit methodology
      b) The auditors
      c) The data
      d) Cost of the audit
H. Appendixes
   1. The social process audit—definition and rationale
   2. Methods used in the audit

Each section of the audit outline should be generally developed in the following manner, always bearing in mind that the specific circumstances surrounding any particular audit may call for some variation from the general format. Regardless of such variations, though, the audit must at a minimum contain the types of information denoted under each major heading if it is to serve the needs of organizational decision makers.

Introduction

The opening section of the audit report should clearly identify the auditors, tell of their professional qualifications for such work, and indicate any organizational relationships they may have, including those with the company being audited.

In addition, it should explain the circumstances under which the decision to undertake the audit was made, so that it will be clear to all who read the audit just where and how the audit has come into existence and where it fits into the organization's authority structure.

The introductory section should also specify the period of time during which the audit was conducted. This information will be particularly useful in those cases where the audited activity is subject to rapid change and where data collected at one point in time may become obsolete.

The Summary Audit Statement

The audit proper should begin with a condensed summary statement of the major findings of the auditors. This condensation is essential in order to give an overview that can be quickly digested before the more detailed information is presented, particularly since the audit will typically set forth carefully developed details about a range of rather complex processes and problems. A simple guide or road map is needed to provide overall directions before the larger mass of information is confronted. Additionally, some organizational managers will not need to concern themselves with all of the detailed information but can profit from an overview. In addition, they will be able to understand and communicate with subordinate personnel charged with responsibility for implementing action in the area that has been audited.

Following this overview of major findings, the auditors' recommendations should be summarized. Once again, it is helpful for responsible officers of the company to grasp the general directions in which changes in practice or policy are being suggested.

These summaries of major findings and of major recommendations should then be keyed with simple page references to the main body of the audit so that anyone interested in a more detailed understanding of some particular part of the audit can find that information with ease.

Presentation of Findings

To give proper perspective for judgment to organizational decision makers, it is important to provide a brief account of how the audited activity came into existence, together with the reasons adduced to justify it then and at present. The auditors' analytic tasks begin just at this point, for embedded in the program's history, sometimes in tangled and unclear fashion, are the original goals as well as the primary motivations that caused the company to embark upon such an activity. Particularly in those instances where voluntary programs are being audited, a historical perspective can be immensely helpful in identifying goals and motivations that may no longer be appropriate to the company's current status. Such is often also the nature of social programs undertaken under the pressure of external social action groups clamoring for action from the organization. Even where a company is forced to enter into social activities by virtue of some government program or legislation, such as pollution control or employment discrimination, the program's history can be useful in revealing changes in attitudes within the company, or modifications in government laws, or constantly changing interpretations of the laws and regulations through regulatory agency rulings or court decisions. One of the prime purposes of the social process audit is to shine a clear light upon the social impacts an organization is having upon its community, and vice versa. Knowing the history of any particular social impact is the beginning of such understanding.

A second step in the presentation of the audit's findings is to identify as clearly as possible and in as great detail as practicable each of the individual focal areas of the audited activity. In Chapter 3, we presented an audit methodology keyed to these focal areas. They include the program's goals, inputs, implementation, and outputs. Insofar as possible, this information should be largely descriptive, leaving for the following section of the audit the analysis of such matters.

Auditors will quickly recognize, however, that such analytic work is necessary in order to arrive at even a simple description of the focal areas. As noted previously, a program's goals may be both formal and informal, openly acknowledged and unconsciously held, organizationally shared and personally pursued. Program goals are typically layered in this fashion, and it is often true that communication about the goals follows this layering. In an antidiscrimination program, for example, the official organizational goal may be to hire, train, and promote employees who have previously experienced discrimination at the hands of that company, while the "real" but unspoken organizational goal is to reduce the likelihood of action by the Equal Employment Opportunity Commission or the Office of Federal Contract Compliance. At the same time, there can be a range of personal goals at work, from a desire on the part of some managers to rectify past practices for moral reasons to others' desires to protect their job security from new potential competitors. Goal identification therefore is no simple matter, and the audit report should make certain that all of these complex possibilities are set forth for full consideration.

Inputs to the social program should be described. These inputs, or resources, include those coming from both inside and outside the organization. The obvious inputs consist of money, personnel time, and various types of administrative overhead expenses. Where a company's social program reaches out to other organizations in the community, as in the case of one of the social audits summarized in the following chapter, both the company and the recipient community organization may make similar types of program inputs, such as direct money allocations, personnel time, and administrative overhead. Regardless of their source, all program inputs that bear directly and importantly upon the activity and that help to make the program possible should be included in the auditors' description. Depending upon how and by whom they are viewed, these inputs to the program may be considered as costs to one organization and as gains to another organization. To the auditors, all such inputs are simply resources devoted to the maintenance of the program. The test for inclusion in the audit is whether the input is undertaken in support of or more generally contributes to the particular company program.

Some of these program inputs may be normally unrecognized or covert in nature. For example, psychological inputs or social attitude inputs may help to sustain a particular program, but their presence may be overlooked. An instance may be found in one of the audits we describe in the next chapter, where the auditors surmise that the administrative personnel in certain community welfare agencies have had to accept a welfare-dependency status vis-a-vis the company that donates products to the agencies. Otherwise, the program could not operate. The auditors note that the acceptance of this inferior social status constitutes a type of psychological cost or input on the part of the agency personnel. At the same time, it should be obvious that any precise measurement or statement of such socio-psychological inputs is extremely difficult and probably impossible. Nevertheless, a general description of this type of program input is possible and desirable for completeness in understanding all of the program's dimensions. Moreover, knowledge about this type of input may be very helpful in improving the effectiveness of the program.

How the program is actually implemented should be set forth carefully by the audit report. Here, an outside team of auditors can often blow a fresh breath of air through a long-established organizational activity, revealing it for what it really is rather than what it is popularly supposed to be. Not only may myths be thereby dispelled, but policy makers and important decision makers may learn things about their organization that they never fully knew.

Though the social audit report needs to be thorough and forthright in describing how the program is operationalized, a precise and careful use of language is counseled in order to protect the organizational sensibilities of those managers responsible for the program. As we pointed out in Chapter 2, organizational politics and executive sensibilities can have important effects, not just upon the implementation of a social audit but also upon how its findings and recommendations will be viewed and treated.

Who does what, how frequently, and with what portion of the available resources or inputs should be spelled out without regard for consistency with or support of the previously identified goals. The purpose here is simply to make clear how the activity is actually pursued. Analysis for consistency follows in the next section.

The same objectively open description of the social program's outputs or results comes next. Once again, outputs may or may not be consistent with those sought or those thought to be the official goals. It is even possible, particularly in the social arena, that the most important program accomplishments will be those most closely related to the informal, covert, or unspoken goals of the program. For example, the positive impact upon the attitudes and morale of disadvantaged employees that may be created when an organization's leading decision makers fully and openly accept an antidiscrimination program may far outweigh in importance the "official" goal of hiring a given percentage of such disadvantaged employees. Social auditors must therefore be alert to these possible program outputs and describe them as fully as they describe the intended and expected accomplishments.

When all of these descriptions and findings related to each of the focal areas have been set forth, the social report can move on to the next section.

Analysis of Program Processes

The social process audit takes its name from the fact that it attempts to describe and analyze a social process. That process consists of a series of inputs and outputs that are related to a goal-oriented program or activity that has identifiable social consequences for the larger community. Since the program's inputs (that is, the resources devoted to it) and outputs (its accomplishments) take place in an ongoing company, that company's traits and characteristics, its policies and goals will affect the social program also. Therefore, the auditors should be prepared to analyze the program's inputs and outputs, as well as those aspects of the company that affect the audited activity.

All of the social and organizational processes that are directly and indirectly involved in the program's operation should be examined with the greatest care. Not only must each of the focal areas mentioned previously be analyzed for adequacy and effectiveness, but they should be related to one another and seen as a whole. For example, resource inputs to a social program (such as pollution control) should be analyzed for their adequacy in attaining a proposed goal (such as a given level of pollution reduction); and an analysis should also be made of the appropriateness of that particular goal itself, given other goals being pursued by the organization. Likewise, a social audit may reveal that a program is being implemented with reasonable effectiveness, given the resource inputs being devoted to it, but that a far greater degree of effectiveness could be achieved by increasing the resource inputs, or focusing on a narrower range of goals.

This is perhaps only another way of saying that social auditors should attempt to avoid the error of suboptimization of goals. A type of systems analysis is called for, in which the auditors try to embrace as many of the social processes at work as feasible. This means that they should not visualize goals as existing in one compartment, inputs in another, implementation efforts in a third, and outputs in a fourth. Once having broken these related social processes down into categories, it is important to return them to their original whole and to describe their relationship to each other.

This section of the audit report should therefore deal directly with the following questions: Are the various formal and informal, organizational and personal, and spoken and unspoken goals of the program being achieved? Are the resource inputs—from the company, from outside organizations, from employees and others—adequate for goal achievement? Is the program being effectively and efficiently implemented, given the array of goals and given existing internal and external resource inputs? Are the program's outputs the intended or expected ones, and are they consistent with recognized goals, the flow of resource inputs earlier identified, and the manner in which the program is being operationalized?

In answering these questions, the audit report is pursuing two related lines of inquiry. First, it seeks to analyze each one of the focal areas—goals, inputs, implementation, and outputs—in terms of adequacy or effectiveness. Second, the analysis then turns to how they are all related to one another. For example, if program outputs are found to be widely inconsistent with recognized program goals, are the inputs inadequate, or is implementation poorly done, or are the goals sought unrealistic? This phase of the analysis and audit report might be dubbed a type of consistency analysis, wherein an effort is made to determine and describe how each of the social processes affects the others and whether they are consistent within themselves in this particular organization at this particular point in time.

Problem Identification and Analysis

From a management point of view, the most important part of a social audit is the identification and analysis of problems associated with the social activity. Here, it is probably true that an external audit team can be more helpful than company insiders by providing a relatively objective and detached view of the activity and its major problems. Here, also, one will find the greatest degree of sensitivity by those responsible for the audited program. Nevertheless, this kind of information is what the social process audit is all about, and the audit report should deal forthrightly with such matters.

This section should be as succinct as possible and should follow the outline of focal areas used previously for identifying and analyzing the program's major components.

Problems may be evident with respect to the goals being pursued. They may be too ambitious or too modest. They may be inconsistent with other more important company goals. They may be outmoded in terms of the current social scene. They may lack integration into the organization's regular policy review practices. On the other hand, of course, they may be just right for the circumstances and the time.

Likewise, program inputs may be inadequate, or due to changed circumstances they may prove to be lavish. The wrong persons or departments may be spending too much time and money on the social program. The recipient agencies, if any, may be found to be grossly inefficient in their use of resources. Employee cooperation, where a social activity is dependent upon such help, may be lacking or sluggish. Any and all such difficulties should be pinpointed by the audit report.

Or the program's major problems may center in the way it is being implemented rather than in its goals and the quality of its inputs. Organizational priorities may be such as to push the social program down to a low level of consideration by managers and support staff preoccupied with other activities. Staff may simply be inadequate in numbers. Poor management may prevail. Communication and feedback mechanisms may well be absent or poorly tended. Whatever the problems, they should be carefully described and analyzed by the auditors.

In similar fashion, the program's outputs may well prove to be the trouble spot. They may be the wrong or unintended accomplishments. In the social arena especially, they may backfire in some unanticipated and (from the company point of view) unrealized fashion. They may merely fall short of what is hoped for. The audit should set them forth clearly.

Finally, at this point in the identification and analysis of problems, the social report should delve into the entire matter of the adequacy of the social data base. Usually, social auditors do not find enough data, and what they find may be quite inadequate for their purposes. As noted in an earlier chapter, there may also be problems of organizational sensitivity and organizational politics that hinder the collection of needed information. Moreover, the auditors may discover that their existing data collection methods are less than able to reveal what they would like to know or that the costs associated with obtaining better quality information are prohibitive. Most of these problems arise during the course of a social process audit, and they should be candidly discussed along with the problems that arise from the operation of the program itself.

Recommendations

At this point in the audit report, the auditors are in position to offer their recommendations to management. With the one important exception of lacking full familiarity with the company's working procedures and organizational attitudes, an outside audit team possesses more information and more insight into the audited activity than will be typically true of most company personnel, often including those in direct charge of the social program. Particularly important is the auditors' overview of the program and its relationship to other company goals and other social impacts that the company may be having on the community. Moreover, it is often but not universally true that social auditors possess professional knowledge about social and community activities that may be quite helpful to organizational decision makers who are typically more familiar with economic and financial matters. At least, the social audit itself has given the auditors a more recent and comprehensive view of this particular social program and its place in the company and in the community than has probably been taken by company management.

The recommendations should follow the same outline used previously with respect to each focal area of the audited activity: the goals and goal conflict, program inputs, implementation, the outputs, and the data base.

We wish to give special emphasis to the latter category of recommendations. Social data requirements can become critically important if the company intends to continue some form of the social audit on a periodic basis, however infrequent. The auditors, better than anyone else, are in a position to describe how better and clearer information can be provided for future audits, together with cost estimates of doing so. We can only repeat what others have often observed—namely, that the typical array of information available for social impact analyses tends to be skimpy. The internal management of a company where these data deficiencies exist should therefore hear from the social auditors themselves what positive steps might be taken to improve this situation.

Audit Evaluation

The audit report should provide an evaluation of the audit itself, particularly in view of the novelty and relatively untried character of some of social auditing's techniques. This evaluation should focus on the limitations of social auditing in general as well as on those experienced in conducting the particular audit being reported.

Included in this section can be a discussion of the shortcomings of any of the audit methodologies used, some indication of the experience and professional backgrounds of the auditors, still another mention of data problems that might have conditioned the analysis or recommendations, and an estimate of the cost of undertaking the audit if there is no commercial transaction involved. The latter cost estimate, which may be made in either hours or monetary terms, can give management as well as the auditors some overall basis for judging the economic feasibility of social auditing.

Appendixes

We believe it is a good idea to include in an appendix a brief and simple description of the social process audit. It could include an indication of the general purpose, methods used, major types of questions asked, special problems often encountered, and what might be expected from the audit. Examples should also be given of the types of social programs and activities that have been audited or could be. Such a description can be useful to those not familiar with the terminology or procedures of social auditing and will better enable readers of the audit to understand it.

For any particular social audit, it is important also to include in a separate appendix detailed information about the methods used in that social audit, together with technical data related to the audited program. Examples would be charts and tables setting forth employment statistics, industrial safety records and forms, community agencies receiving philanthropic contributions, program cost data, and so on.

A CONCLUDING COMMENT

As noted at the beginning of this chapter, the whole purpose of the social process audit is to provide organizational decision makers with enough information about a particular social program or activity to enable them either to reaffirm or to modify the company's social practices and policies. Although the format suggested here has proved to be a workable one in our experience and one that has been useful for management review, the particular form followed is less important than the content of the social audit. The social report to management, like all management reports, should be clear, to the point, and useful. Anything less leaves the organization and its major decision makers open to needless criticism and misunderstanding as a result of misconceptions about the company's social impacts.

6

CASE STUDIES:
TWO SOCIAL PROCESS
AUDITS

This chapter presents the major portions of two social process audits conducted for a large corporation by the Social Audit Research Group of the University of Pittsburgh. The names of the company and its personnel are omitted, as are all dollar figures and numbers. These omissions do not affect the purpose of this chapter, which is to illustrate what a social process audit is and how it is presented.

In its original form, each audit was approximately 100 typed pages long. For this chapter, the information appearing in individual sections has been considerably condensed, but each section heading that appears in the audit is shown here in the proper sequence.

The first audit is that of a philanthropic contributions program through which the company makes donations of its product to certain welfare agencies in the minority community in which it is headquartered. The second is an audit of a safety program in one plant of the same company. While the overall format is the same for both audits, differences in the programs being audited dictate corresponding differences in the reports, thereby providing two contrasting examples of social process audits.

Both of these programs have undergone significant change in the interim since they were audited. A number of problems identified by the social audit team, as well as some of the recommendations, have been recognized and acted upon by company management. Not all of these changes can be traced directly to the social audits themselves inasmuch as some modifications were already under way at the time. Nevertheless, the audits have provided a more comprehensive and systematic overview of the two programs, their accomplishments, and their limitations than had previously been available.

In order to preserve the original form and content of the two social audits, while simultaneously recognizing and identifying the company's progress in making needed changes, an epilogue has been appended to each of the audits. The separate epilogues provide an updating of each program since originally audited, thereby giving a more complete picture of the company's efforts and activities in each of these areas of social action.

A SOCIAL AUDIT OF
A CONTRIBUTIONS PROGRAM
ADMINISTERED BY THE ____ COMPANY
FOR SELECTED LOCAL COMMUNITY AGENCIES

Prepared by the Social Audit Research Group,
Graduate School of Business, University of Pittsburgh

I. Introduction

In March 197_ representatives of the Social Audit Research Group at the University of Pittsburgh were invited to meet with company officials for purposes of discussing various company programs where a social audit would be useful to management. One of the programs identified was a philanthropic contributions program, and the social audit was begun during that same month.

The Social Audit Research Group is composed of faculty members and advanced doctoral students from the Graduate School of Business at the University of Pittsburgh. Three of its members are responsible for the audit of the contributions program.

It should be noted that the Social Audit Research Group (SARG) operates as a nonprofit informal organization of individual faculty members and students, that the members of SARG are solely responsible for the contents and views expressed herein, that none of the contents represents official views of the Graduate School of Business or of the University of Pittsburgh, and that neither SARG nor any of its individual members has received any monetary or other compensation from the company for conducting this social audit.

In accordance with the agreement reached at the outset of the study, this social audit report is submitted to the general manager, Communications.

II. Summary Audit Statement

This section contains a summary of the major findings, conclusions, and recommendations of the social audit. Further details concerning each major point can be found in later sections, as indicated by the numbers of the respective sections enclosed in parentheses.

The Program

The program consists of the provision by the company of merchandise distributed free of charge on a monthly basis to approximately 19 community agencies in minority-community neighborhoods. The program is directed by the general manager, Communications. The annual budget is approximately $____ (III).

The Goals of the Program

The company's goals for the program are (1) to provide free merchandise to meet the critical needs of selected community agencies, (2) to improve relations with the minority community by demonstrating that the company is a good corporate citizen, and (3) to keep program costs at a minimal level (III).

The program's administrative staff's goals are (1) to help the company to be a socially responsible company, (2) to extend the company's public relations function to the minority community, and (3) to gain personal satisfaction from helping to fulfill a perceived community need (III).

The recipient agencies' goals are (1) to obtain limited amounts of free merchandise to supplement slim agency budgets, and (2) possibly to test the company's goodwill and general attitude toward the minority community (III).

The Resource Inputs to the Program

Company inputs to the program include the direct costs of the merchandise, administrative costs, and overhead charges totalling approximately $____ per year, plus approximately ___ employee-days per year (III).

Community agency inputs to the program include direct pickup and transportation costs ranging from $____ to $____ per year per agency, plus the agency's administrative staff time in handling and accounting for the merchandise, plus agency overhead. In addition, a psychological cost of unknown and unmeasurable dimensions is incurred by agency personnel in assuming a welfare-dependency status vis-a-vis the company (III).

The Results of the Program Regarding Company Goals:

(1) The program is moderately successful in helping the recipient agencies meet their emergency needs, but, though useful, the amount of assistance provided by the program is marginal and minimal (IV).

(2) The program probably improves the company's image in the minority community among a very small number of persons who know about the program (IV).

(3) The above two goals are being achieved to the extent indicated above at a marginal cost to the company (IV).

Regarding the Program's Administrative Staff's Goals:

(1) Given the modest size of the program, it is doubtful that much could be claimed for the company's socially responsible posture as a result of this effort, which is marginal in terms of some of the specific problems of the minority community and in terms of the company's resources (IV).

(2) The program does help fulfill the normal public relations function of the Communications Department (IV).

(3) The program is apparently successful in providing the administrative staff with a personal satisfaction that an important community need is being partially met (IV).

Regarding the Community Agencies' Goals:

(1) The recipient agencies are receiving limited amounts of merchandise for emergency needs and are generally satisfied and grateful (IV).

(2) It is not possible to state whether the agencies' overall attitude toward the company is positive or negative as a result of this program, but there is some evidence to suggest that those minority-community persons familiar with the program hold positive views toward the company (IV).

Problems of the Program With Respect to the Program Goals:

(1) The personal goals of the program's administrative staff tend to dominate the program, as opposed to organizational commitment and formal review by higher administrative authority (V).

(2) The modest size of the program's budget exposes the company to a potential charge of "corporate tokenism," and this could negate efforts and intentions to cultivate a positive company image in the minority community (V).

(3) The program, in being geared to meeting emergency needs by means of a standard package of merchandise, cannot provide either flexibility or breadth in meeting the special needs of the recipient agencies (V).

With Respect to Resource Inputs:

(1) The administrative staff, though well motivated and possessing experience in handling this program, lacks formal training in dealing with complex urban community problems and has little significant continuing contact with the minority community (V).

(2) The administrative personnel of the community agencies received little or no advice or training in the use of the merchandise (V).

With Respect to Administration and Implementation:

(1) The criteria used for selection and retention of community agencies in the program are too personalized, and the guidelines are therefore not clear (V).

(2) The contents of the standard package of merchandise are not always consistent with recipient agency needs, and at times the contents of the packages may vary in apparently arbitrary ways (V).

(3) The organizational control and feedback system exhibits deficiencies regarding the quality of merchandise delivered, an absence of follow-up checks on how the agencies have utilized the products, and the lack of an effective communication system from the community agencies to the company (V).

Recommendations

First, the company should review the program's goals and:

(1) Consider formalizing the program's goals through periodic review and evaluation of the goals and results achieved (VI).

(2) Consider alternative or additional goals, such as a flexible content for the merchandise packages, assisting other types of agencies, or focusing company resources on a single agency or a single type of agency (VI).

Second, the company should increase the amounts and quality of its monetary and personnel inputs by:

(1) Training key administrative personnel associated with the program in urban community problems (VI).

(2) Providing advice and training in the use of the merchandise to community agency personnel (VI).

Third, the company should improve administration and implementation of the program by:

(1) Formalizing the criteria for selection and retention of community agencies (VI).

(2) Supplementing the present management control and communication system in ways that will insure closer supervision of the program within the company and a freer flow of communication from the recipient agencies to the company (VI).

III. Major Findings

Description of the Program

The program described is one of three donation programs that the company manages. All are voluntary philanthropic activities on the part of the company. The program is permanent and continuous in that it provides products to recipient organizations on a regular monthly basis. It resembles a wholesaler-retailer arrangement where the company restocks its customers on a regular or periodic basis to keep their inventories at an adequate level. There are 19 recipient organizations.

The program was started locally, at the company's headquarters, and no similar programs exist at other company locations. Administrative responsibility and the organization of the program are under the direct control of the general manager of the Communications Department, who reports to a vice president. The manager's responsibilities relative to the program include general administrative and supervisory duties with the ultimate authority to add or delete recipient organizations and make changes in the kinds of products going to these groups. Matters concerning the program are only a small part of his overall responsibilities. When the program first began in the late 1960s, however, it took considerably more of his time since he delivered the products personally to the organizations.

The principal staff person in the program is the associate manager of Consumer Relations who reports to the general manager, Communications. The associate manager has a staff of four in that department, and the department as a whole spends only about four days a month on matters related to this program. Their responsibilities are strictly related to the implementation of the program and do not involve authorization of organizations or of items for delivery.

New organizations that want to become a part of the program specify their purpose and reasons for wanting to become involved in a letter (Appendix 6.D). The Communications manager then makes an informal check of the organization through his own contacts in the minority community and his staff people who may know the organization. His decision as to whether or not an organization becomes part of the program is final. Once an organization enters the program, 12 requisitions (one for each month of the year) are typed and placed on file by the Consumer Relations Department, which is responsible for ongoing implementation of the program.

The Consumer Relations Department also maintains a file of recipient activity, and from time to time the associate manager suggests dropping organizations that have been relatively inactive (Appendix 6.D). The department also keeps a running inventory record (Appendix 6.D) of the stock that is available in the warehouse for filling requests.

The only other staff people directly involved in the program are warehouse personnel when the products are picked up by the recipient organizations. The recipient organizations have to call the Consumer Relations Department once each month to declare their intention of picking up that month's allotment. Once the call is received, a requisition is sent to the warehouse where the requested products are set aside from a stock maintained by the warehouse personnel for the program. Usually three days' lead time is needed between the call and the actual pickup. The cost of this particular program to the company is modest. The standard package is supposed to be first-rate merchandise and not surplus. While some organizations place 12 orders a year, others do not make requests this frequently, and the total merchandise costs have been estimated at $____ per year over the last five years.

Origin and Development of the Program

The program began at the time when riots were frequent in minority communities throughout the country, and these were a definite influence on the development of the program. Thus, the program was in large part a response to these pressures from within the minority community. The company made an attempt to look at the total problems in the minority community, and the program was part of a broader response to these problems. Since rioting and other forms of group violence have largely subsided within minority communities in recent years, these can no longer be considered an active external influence.

Other companies within the industry have also had an influence on the program. Some seemed to be getting better publicity about their social concern, so this company may have felt some competitive pressure. Also, when the program was first conceived, the existence of a related program in another company gave great encouragement.

The program was started a little more than five years ago (1968) by the then manager of Public Relations for the company. Later, when he became general manager of Communications, the program came under his direction and remains part of his responsibility (although there was one other manager in the interim).

The original objectives of the program were to provide aid on a continuing basis to family and children's service organizations to help them meet any critical situations they might encounter. These objectives have since been broadened to include drug rehabilitation agencies but the majority of the recipient organizations are still of the family and children's service type.

This program fits into the general company philosophy of helping the community and maintaining good community relations. Thus, when minority problems became a national issue in the 1960s, it seemed natural to expect that the company would be involved in dealing with these problems in some fashion.

The program has probably tripled in size since its beginnings, based upon the dollar value of merchandise provided to recipient organizations. Until 1973, money for the program came out of the Communications manager's departmental budget. Funding now comes out of the company's general contributions budget, but the reasons for this change were not explained to the social audit team.

Communications policies over the years have been directed toward maintaining a low profile for the program. There was a news release about the program several years ago and an article in an employee publication, but the assumption is that word-of-mouth communicates the essentials of such a program better than the media and at the same time minimizes the danger of being deluged with requests from other community agencies.

Until 1974, there apparently was no formal evaluation of the program's effects. Whatever evaluation that did take place previously was of an informal and casual type, relying primarily on telephone conversations with the recipient organizations.

This program is continued because of the personal interest of the communications manager and involved staff. While organizational awareness of the program certainly extends to the vice president to whom the Communications manager reports and may extend to the company's president, motivation for continuing the program comes from the Communications manager and department staff. Thus, the program was originally started and is continued because of interest at lower levels of the organization rather than at the top level.

Major Program Components: Goals and Objectives

Company Goals. (1) From the company's viewpoint, this program is designed to meet critical needs of people in the poorer parts of the minority community as these needs are perceived by the recipient agencies. It is geared to provide for temporary and emergency needs that arise from some crisis situation.

(2) As far as benefits to the company itself are concerned, the goals are to improve relations between the company and the minority community and to present the company as an organization concerned with the well-being of the minority community.

(3) This program also helps to continue the philanthropic traditions of the company.

(4) Another company goal is to achieve all of the above goals at very low marginal cost to the company.

Goals of the Program's Staff. (1) The program helps the company to be a socially responsible organization. The Communications manager personally believes in the concept of social responsibility and feels that this program gives the company an opportunity to do something for low-income or disadvantaged people as part of its broader responsibility to society that goes beyond the production of goods and services.

(2) The program also helps to fulfill an organizationally assigned public relations function.

(3) Other staff goals have to do with the fulfillment of strongly held personal convictions regarding selected minority-community needs. While employee goals may be difficult to assess, it seems clear that the principal staff persons involved in the program derive a great deal of personal satisfaction out of their participation.

Community-Agency Goals. (1) One obvious goal of the agencies is to obtain limited amounts of free merchandise. Personnel at the agencies that were visited expressed a strong desire to continue the program.

(2) Perhaps an inferred goal on the part of the agencies is to test the attitude and good-will of the company toward the minority community. Such "testing" of a company's general posture concerning the welfare of the minority community was perhaps more typical of the immediate postriot period than now. It is suggested here only as a possible, inferred goal.

It can be seen that all of these goals and objectives are diverse in nature. There are formally stated goals and informal goals. There are company goals versus personal goals. There are internal goals of the company and staff versus the external goals of the recipient organizations. Finally, there are economic goals such as maintaining a minimal cost versus the social goals of meeting emergency needs in the minority community. Some of these goals are consistent with each other, others are in conflict. This diverse character of the goals must be kept in mind when assessing how well the goals are being accomplished.

Major Program Components: Resource Inputs

The cost of the merchandise given to the recipient organizations is estimated to be $____ per year. Other company inputs consist of the cost of adding a new organization, which the program's staff estimates to be $____ per organization. The direct cost here consists of paperwork and the time spent in checking out a new organization. Other company inputs are administrative overhead items such as office space, filing space, telephone usage, cost of forms, and warehousing. Cost estimates for these items were not available.

Employee inputs consist of the time spent in administering the program. The department spends about four days per month on matters concerning this program. The only other employee input is the time spent by the warehouse personnel, which is estimated at about five hours per month. Costs were not available in the form of dollar figures for any of these employee inpts, but such computations could be made easily.

Other company inputs are overhead costs—items such as light, heat, insurance, and so on—that should be allocated on some realistic basis to the program. These costs are probably insignificant in amount, and they are not accounted for in any formal sense, but they should at least in principle be recognized as inputs to the program.

Company inputs for which no cost can be assigned either in terms of dollars or time include intangibles such as the social interest and dedication of the program's administrative staff and their organizational superiors. Interest in the program is very high on the part of those most directly responsible for it, and their commitment represents an important company input.

Since the recipients themselves pick up the merchandise from the warehouse, this represents the most significant noncompany input. The direct costs of this activity were $____ per year as reported by the recipients. Other noncompany inputs consist of personnel time spent by the organizations in making contacts with the company to request the monthly order, managing the pickup and delivery, and allocating the merchandise within the organization itself. There are also unallocated overhead costs similar to those mentioned earlier.

The recipient agencies also make intangible inputs. These concern the attitudes and frustrations of the agency personnel in not getting enough merchandise to meet their needs or enough of the right kind for some specialized needs they may have. Beyond this, there has to be a willingness on the part of the agencies to assume a welfare-dependency status vis-a-vis the company. There is surely some input here in terms of the insecurity they feel at the possibility of being cut off from a much needed source of supply and having no recourse other than an appeal to the general good will of the company. In other words, the agencies and their personnel are making a type of psychological investment by virtue of agreeing to participate in the program.

Operational Results of the Program

As stated previously, 19 organizations receive merchandise through this program. A list appears in Appendix 6.D. A questionnaire was sent to these organizations to get some idea of what they were like and how they felt about the program. The response rate was disappointing, but the results were tabulated and appear in Appendix 6.D. In addition, field visits were made to some of the agencies.

Those recipients who responded were satisfied with the program as it presently exists, even to the extent of approving the present delivery system. They have no trouble contacting the right people at the company and feel their requests are handled courteously, promptly, and fairly. Participation in the program has generally made them feel more positive toward this company and toward corporations in general.

While the recipient agency attitudes toward this program and toward the company are generally positive, they seem to be under no delusions about corporate "good-will." The persons interviewed believed that "maybe they do want to help some," but they also thought that perhaps the company used the program as a tax write-off or to dispose of surplus merchandise.

Another operational result of the program concerns the morale of the company's administrative staff, which is high in regard to the program's goals and results. Both of the principal staff persons involved are satisfied with the structure and implementation of the present program and would not change it in any major fashion. Perhaps it can be concluded that the program is presently serving their personal goals adequately.

The program has moved from individualized interest and administration toward organizational acceptance and approval, but this development is not complete. There is no formal budget or program review beyond the Communications manager. Money allocated for this program is absorbed in the total contributions budget and only appears as a line item there. The manager makes the decisions relative to the program budget, taking into account his other responsibilities, which gives him virtually complete control over the program. He expressed the desire to make the budget-setting process more formalized by involving people higher up in the organization, since he feels that budget approval is now more a matter of default than anything else. But in the absence of formal review processes, the problem of personalized goals versus organizational goals is still a factor, as discussed in another section of this report.

IV. Analysis of Goals, Inputs, and Operational Results

Analysis of Goal Achievement

With respect to the first company goal of meeting emergency needs of people in the minority community, this is being accomplished at least on a small scale. Products are being provided to help a handful of people meet a crisis situation. But more remains to be done to meet this objective to any significant degree. Not only is there a great need for more of the same kind of products, but some important needs are not being met, such as certain types of merchandise that are needed by specific agencies.

Regarding the second goal of improving relations with the minority community and presenting the company as being concerned with the well-being of the minority community, there is some evidence to suggest that this is being accomplished. However, there is a question as to how many people know about the donations. There is apparently no general knowledge among the residents at one recipient agency that some of the products they use have been provided by this company free of charge. Only the staff people who receive the products and those involved in picking them up know about the program. It is not clear that knowledge of the company's involvement in this effort is very widespread in the minority community, and this, of course, affects the accomplishment of this goal.

There seems to be no question that the other company goals are being accomplished. Certainly this program continues the philanthropic traditions of the company. And it certainly does not cost the company very much. Whatever other goals are being accomplished are also being reached at low marginal cost to the company.

Regarding staff goals, there is a serious question as to how much the program is helping the company to be a socially responsible organization. One can ask whether the modest expenditure of $____ per year represents a diligent effort to provide a meaningful solution to a social problem of great magnitude. The program does help to fulfill an organizationally assigned public relations function, as mentioned earlier, and also contributes to the fulfillment of the staff's strongly held personal convictions regarding the needs of the minority community.

The agencies are receiving limited amounts of free merchandise, and thus one of their goals is being accomplished. But how well their inferred goals of testing the attitude and good-will of the company toward the minority community are being achieved is open to question. The program is not big enough to represent a significant expression of good-will, and yet its continuance beyond the immediate motivation of the riots may demonstrate that the company has some kind of ongoing concern for the minority community. The audit team does not know whether or to what extent the affected members of the minority community may hold such favorable views of the company.

Analysis of the Adequacy of Resource Inputs

In Terms of the Goals Sought. Taking into account all the company goals, one can say that the program as presently structured does achieve a good balance between them and in this sense the resource inputs are adequate for company purposes.

The present resources are also adequate to meet the needs of the community agencies to obtain limited amounts of free merchandise; however, there are some needs that are not being met even within the size limitations of the program. For example, the inflexibility of the program with respect to the products available in the standard package renders the resources inadequate to deal with the needs, which are of a special nature.

The resources are apparently adequate to meet most of the staff goals. Perhaps one can conclude from this that both personal and organizational needs of company personnel are being met by the current resources. But the resources do not seem adequate in helping the company to be a socially responsible organization. They are too meager to do much toward solving any but a very small set of the overall needs and problems of this kind faced by the minority community.

In Terms of Operational and Organizational Results. Generally, the answer is positive in terms of the operational results achieved. Merchandise is being delivered, and it meets some real needs of the community agencies. The community agencies are positive about the program even though there are some obvious problems with it. The same positive attitude was expressed by the staff relative to their feelings about the program. Thus, the present resources committed to the program seem to be achieving some positive operational results.

Whether the resources committed are adequate in relation to other programs that are a part of community and public relations cannot be analyzed because the figures are unavailable. The inability to perform an opportunity cost analysis must also be noted. Perhaps the resources committed to this program could be better used elsewhere and achieve better results in terms of meeting the goals of all parties concerned.

Relation of Operational Results to Program Goals. As noted above, there is a reasonable consistency between the goals sought by the company, by the administrative personnel, and by the recipient agencies, and the actual results achieved by the program. This suggests that in general the program is successfully administered and implemented in accordance with its goals.

Certain problems associated with the administration and implementation of the program are discussed in the following section.

Problems

Problems with Respect to Goals and Objectives

As noted in the preceding section, this program appears to be successfully achieving its declared goals. The audit has revealed some signs that the company's image is helped in small ways through the program. The recipient agencies gain tangible benefits from it. Its cost is economically marginal to the company. However, two problems should be noted:

Personal Versus Organizational Goals. The past history and present administration of the program reveal that the personal views and social philosophies of its key administrative personnel tend to dominate the setting of the program's goals and objectives. There appears to be little or no formal or explicit review of these goals by higher administrative authority. Some questions may therefore be asked about the appropriateness of such an obvious mixture of personal and organizational goals, without periodic formal review.

For example, what would be the community relations implications for the company if someone less socially aware than the present Communications manager were in charge of the program? What would that imply for the recipient community agencies and their clientele? Does the company want to place itself in the position of depending largely if not solely upon the personal commitment of one person and a dedicated staff in dealing with a community situation that could conceivably erupt to the detriment of the company's image and reputation? Does it wish to leave such fundamental matters as the welfare of the clientele of recipient agencies to the personal views and attitudes of the administrative staff? Would the company not be more assured of achieving its objectives and the recipient agencies be more secure in the long run if ways were found to formalize the personal elements in the present goals and transform them into more settled routines subject to periodic review?

Size of Program Budget. In both absolute and relative terms, the budget for the program is a modest one—approximately $____ annually. At one level, this amount of money seems sufficient to accomplish the program's goals, as noted above.

At another level, though—one dealing with community attitudes toward the company—it may be possible that the very modest size of the budget for this particular program potentially exposes the company to charges of indulging in corporate tokenism and public relations gestures, whereas a primary company goal is to project an attitude of genuine concern and to provide for genuine needs.

The social audit team uncovered no tangible evidence that such negative and potentially harmful community attitudes exist. However, the general area of community attitudes is a notoriously shifting and transitory one, where rapid changes can occur.

Problems with Respect to Resource Inputs

In overall magnitude, the monetary resources devoted to the program appear to be adequate to achieve reasonable success in gaining the major objectives. However, two questions may be raised about the quality of some of the resource inputs:

Lack of Professional Training in Urban Community Problems. The administrative personnel responsible for the program collectively possess many years of experience in dealing with a wide variety of problems in the community relations field. Moreover, their attitudes toward and concern about the problems of the minority community are positive, genuine, and deeply held. However, it should be noted that none of the present administrative staff is professionally trained in the matters dealt with by the recipient community agencies, nor in analyzing and understanding the complexities of contemporary urban problems, nor do they have significant continuing contacts with minority-community members or institutions. With few exceptions, the staff consists of members of the majority community.

Therefore, there may well be a significant gap between the well-founded skills and pragmatic experience accumulated in the program's administrative staff, on the one hand, and the range of knowledge and experience in analyzing contemporary urban processes and problems being accumulated by professionals working in various urban fields of endeavor. Exposing the administrative staff to some of the latter viewpoints and perspectives would help to reduce the size of that gap and would probably enhance the quality of one type of resource input into the program.

Lack of Advice and Training for the Recipient Agency Personnel. The program presently provides for no explicit advice or training in the use of the products for administrative personnel of the recipient agencies. The absence of such advice or training is consistent with the program's main objective of simply providing given quantities of merchandise to the agencies.

However, two considerations suggest the possible worthwhileness of adding such an element. First, the efficiency with which the recipient agencies utilize the merchandise might be enhanced, thereby contributing to greater achievements of the program's goals of supplementing the needs of the agencies' clienteles. Second, with the rising public interest in consumer matters generally, the simple provision of merchandise may in time be perceived as an inadequate objective of the program from the viewpoint of the recipient agencies.

Problems with Respect to Administration and Implementation

Criteria for Selecting Recipient Agencies. The reasons for selecting the recipient community agencies are not always clear and appear to follow no systematic set of criteria. Historically, these selection criteria seem to be a function of the personal values of the program's administrators and their collective knowledge of the minority community. To some extent, selection depends upon initiatives taken by agencies to identify their needs to the company. The social audit team was not able to determine with any specificity the guidelines used to make final selections of agencies.

Contents of the Standard Package. Two kinds of problems arise with respect to the standard package. First and most important, the contents are not necessarily consistent with the precise needs of the various recipient agencies. A second problem is either (1) that the standard package content is not standard but varies from time to time, or (2) that warehouse personnel are substituting one type of product for another when the packages are picked up. The social audit team discovered only one example of this, but its occurrence raises the possibility that other nonstandard items are delivered from time to time.

Organizational Control and Feedback System. Several factors suggest a weakness in the system for controlling the program's activities and keeping management informed about the extent to which the program is meeting its intended objectives.

First, the warehouse sometimes provides to the recipient agencies packages that convey the impression of being second-class merchandise. The program's administrators have not been aware of this apparent breakdown in their plans and expectations that recipient agencies are to receive first-class merchandise identical to that sold in commercial channels.

Second, there is little or no formal check by the company to establish the identity or proper authorization of the persons who call in and pick up the packages for the recipient agencies.

Third, there is no formal administrative review of the results achieved within the recipient agency through delivery of the packages. While no evidence exists to indicate that the merchandise is not being used for official purposes, it remains true that the program's administrators have no systematic way to establish whether diversion of merchandise to other purposes occurs.

Fourth, there is no established, easy way for the recipient agencies to communicate with the program's administrators regarding their special problems and needs or to indicate approval and satisfaction with the program. Prevailing attitudes and traditions within the program tend to discourage this kind of systematic feedback. By failing to have a formal and expected system for hearing both criticism and praise from the recipient agencies, the program's administrators are foregoing opportunities for building more good-will relationships in the community as well as depriving themselves of information about how and whether the program is achieving its objectives.

VI. Recommendations

Recommendations About Goals and Objectives

The company should undertake a careful review of its goals and objectives in sponsoring this program, with special attention to the following factors:

1. The positive and negative factors associated with maintaining the present mixture of personal values and company interests that characterizes the

program and its administration, as discussed above. Although personal values cannot and need not be ignored in setting program goals, a formal administrative, periodic review of program goals would provide an organizational safeguard for the company.

2. Consideration of possible alternative ways of simultaneously helping to meet the various needs of the recipient agencies and their clienteles and to promote the company's reputation within the minority community. The following possibilities are listed in order of their importance and priority, as viewed by the social audit team:

First, either within the limitations of the present budget or with an expanded budget, provide quantities or types of merchandise differing from those found in the standard package. A flexible content is preferable and more consistent with agency needs.

Second, provide on a regular and continuing basis skilled professional service and training of agency personnel in various aspects of the use of the products.

Third, add other types of community agencies to the list receiving the packages.

Fourth, consider concentrating company resources available for these purposes either on a single community agency or on a class of community agency as a demonstration project or as a model of corporation-community cooperation, rather than spreading the present budget over a larger number of agencies.

3. Although this audit is limited to one program, a thorough-going review by the company of its goals and objectives for this particular program would obviously include consideration of related company activities, such as other types of philanthropic contributions or other company actions with community relations implications that bear some relation to the company's image within the region. Such a review might either sustain or call into question this program.

Recommendations about Resource Inputs

Depending upon decisions made as a result of the review of goals and objectives recommended above, the company should increase its monetary and personnel inputs to the program in a variety of ways.

First, some steps should be taken to train key administrative personnel associated with the program in the major aspects of urban problems, racial attitudes and problems, and so on.

Second, with an expanded set of goals, properly trained personnel from the company should be assigned to the program to give technical advice to the agencies regarding use of the merchandise.

Recommendations About Administration and Implementation

Regarding administration and implementation of the program, the following steps should be taken:

1. The criteria used for the selection and retention of community agencies should be depersonalized.

2. The program's control and feedback system should be strengthened in the following ways:

First, take steps to ensure that only first-class merchandise is used.

Second, devise a system to ensure that properly authorized personnel from the recipient agencies pick up the packages and actually deliver them to their intended destination.

Third, actively encourage the recipient agencies to communicate on a regular basis with the program's administrative personnel. The company, not the agency, has the obligation to establish and actively promote this type of communication.

VII. Limitations of the Audit

The validity of this social audit is limited by a number of factors.

The Newness of Social Auditing. The entire field of social auditing is relatively new. The particular form of social audit used here—called the social process audit—is a newly developed managerial tool. Its systematic use in corporations has been quite limited to date. For these reasons and because there remains much developmental work yet to be done to perfect the underlying concepts, methods, and procedures of social auditing, a more than usual caution should be exercised in drawing conclusions based upon this particular audit.

Limitations of the Social Audit Research Group. Three limitations should be noted regarding the Social Audit Research Group and the three-person social audit team that conducted this audit.

First, although the group is one of only a small handful of professional groups in the nation actually conducting social audits within companies, its personnel nevertheless are new to the field and relatively inexperienced in such work. The fact that most others are also inexperienced, perhaps even to a greater degree, does not remove this factor as a limitation of the audit.

Second, as noncompany personnel, the social audit team lacks a thorough knowledge of the company, its procedures, and policies. Its judgments may therefore be wide of the mark in some instances, although it does possess the advantage of a detached and disinterested noncompany view in conducting the social audit.

Third, the audit has been made on a part-time basis over an extended period of time and therefore has not received the intensity of attention that could be achieved by full-time people. In this respect, though, the relationship is not dissimilar to those often experienced with other types of consultancy arrangements.

Limitations of the Data. There were no serious problems regarding the data provided by the company, either as to its quantity or quality, nor were there problems of access to the program's personnel or records.

On the other hand, reliable, verifiable information about the impact of the program on the recipient community agencies, their administrative personnel, and especially their clienteles is seriously limited.

Limitations of Method. Two limitations of method should be noted:

First, a quantitatively expressed cost-benefit analysis of the program is not possible because some important elements and results of the program are not quantifiable. However, this particular limitation does not prevent careful and systematic analysis of the program's goals, resource applications, both quantitative and qualitative results, and the possible future consequences of the program for the company.

Second, neither is it possible to undertake a quantitative analysis of the program's opportunity costs (that is, the range of possible other benefits to be derived from this program's resources if they were to be applied in other ways). This leaves informed executive judgment as the main means of making budgetary allocation decisions concerning the program.

Potential Cost Limitations. Social auditing is complex, time-consuming work. It is conservatively estimated that 170 person-hours were expended on this audit. Three persons were involved in the field study on a part-time basis over a period of approximately 12 months, plus additional time to write the audit report. Since the work of the Social Audit Research Group is funded by grants from a private foundation, the company has not incurred any direct monetary costs of any kind for this audit.

However, in a case similar to this one where the program being audited has a small budget, the economic costs of the audit (if done on a commercial basis) would probably outweigh the economic benefits to the company. The extent to which this cost factor is thought to be a limitation upon social auditing in the future depends upon a company judgment about the usefulness of the information reported in the audit.

In making such a judgment, the company should consider more than economic costs and benefits alone. A systematically developed knowledge of community attitudes resulting from such a program, especially where issues and attitudes can quickly escalate into major company problems, is valuable to management.

Appendix 1 The Social Process Audit: Definition and Rationale

[The material in this Appendix is a condensation of pages 10-20 in Chapter 1 of this book. Its purpose is to provide a quick overview of the social process audit for those unfamiliar with it.]

Appendix 2 Outline of a Social Process Audit Methodology

[The materials in Chapters 3 and 4 are condensed to give a general view of the approach used, the types of information sought, and the kinds of analyses employed.]

Appendix 3 Methods Used in this Audit

[The primary methods used in this particular audit were the following: examination of company records, questionnaires, and interviews. This Appendix explains how each of these methods was used in the audit and includes copies of interview schedules and questionnaires.]

Appendix 4 Exhibits—Charts—Tabulated Data

[Company organization charts, sample letters, forms, and records, and questionnaire results are duplicated in this Appendix.]

Epilogue and Update

In the interim since this audit was undertaken, a number of changes have been made in this program. Several of these modifications are consistent with recommendations made by the social audit team, although some of them were already contemplated and under way prior to submission of the social audit to the company's management. They are identified here in order to give a more complete picture of the program and to indicate the practical usefulness of a social audit in assessing a given program.

Administrative Staff for the Program. Perhaps of foremost importance is the presence of a full-time Community Relations coordinator who is responsible, among other activities, for this particular program and who reports to the general manager, Communications. The Community Relations coordinator is a minority person with some ten years' experience in urban affairs and with a professional background appropriate to the technical use of the products contributed through this program.

Additionally, the Community Relations coordinator and staff now spend about six days a month on this particular program, as contrasted with the four days previously reported in the audit.

Evaluation, Control, and Communication. A formal budget and program review is now periodically made by the Community Relations coordinator and the general manager, Communications, thus replacing the informal review previously made and tending to alleviate the problems posed by reliance upon a system of informal, personalized goals and criteria.

An improved control and feedback system is now in operation, ensuring proper control over merchandise pickup and encouraging recipient agencies to communicate more freely with the company regarding their reactions to the program.

Expanded Agency List. Since the audit was conducted, a number of agencies have been added to those receiving merchandise, thereby extending the reach of the program into the community. A total of 22 agencies of four types are now served, including welfare and family service organizations, drug rehabilitation centers, the Salvation Army, and community centers.

* * *

In an overall sense, this program is only one of several philanthropic activities of the company, which has a long history of concern for its employees, customers, and the general community. Though relatively modest in size, this particular program's impact should be judged as part of a more comprehensive set of activities intended to improve the communities in which the company does business.

A SOCIAL AUDIT OF
THE SAFETY PROGRAM OF THE ___ COMPANY

Prepared by
the Social Audit Research Group, Graduate School of Business,
University of Pittsburgh

I: Summary Audit Statement

The Summary Audit Statement is a summary presentation of the major findings, conclusions, and recommendations which resulted from the Social Audit Research Group's "process audit" of the safety program.

The process audit involved a number of specific areas of investigation, including: historical perspective and rationale; goals; inputs; implementation; outputs of the safety program. Data were collected through interviews with headquarters management and with management, supervisors, and hourly employees at one plant. Additional insights were gained through participant observation of the program as it operated and through analysis of available records.

The process audit analysis seeks to examine the safety program as it operates in order to better enable management to determine the directions the program might take in the future. The analysis considers both management's views as to how the program should operate and the auditors' views as to how it actually does operate. Points of consistency and possible conflict among elements within the program are identified and recommended actions put forth. Parenthetical citations are for specific parts of the Audit Report which further elaborate on the points made in the statement.

Analysis of Program

Historical Perspective. Much greater attention is presently accorded to safety than in the past (II). The Occupational Safety and Health Act of 1970 (OSHA) corresponds approximately to the beginnings of this increased attention (II).

Rationale for Program. Economic: effective program will lead to increased employee morale, improved production, insurance savings (II, III). *Moral:* headquarters management is humanely concerned for the safety and welfare of all personnel and would actively take steps to provide for their safety regardless of possible economic justifications (II).

Goals. Safety is said to be a major company goal, ranking with production, quality, and sales (II). Headquarters management views an accident-free environment as the ultimate or ideal goal of the program (II).

Operational Sub-Goals. Complete compliance with OSHA (II). Reduction of company-wide lost-time-accident (L.T.A.) injury rate (II). Attitude change toward increased safety consciousness of all personnel (II).

Analysis. In the plant, L.T.A. reduction is widely viewed as *the* safety goal (II, III). Management's humane concern for employees is not generally perceived; increased management attention to safety is attributed largely to OSHA (II, III). Increased safety consciousness is not readily noticeable, except among members of the factory safety committee (II). The importance of safety as a goal has not been well communicated (II, III). Personnel below plant manager were uncertain as to how safety performance specifically affected overall performance rating (II).

Inputs. Resources are almost wholly provided by the company; little use is made of noncompany or employee resources (II). The use of personnel time is perceived by management as an increasingly important means of improving safety effectiveness and of improving safety awareness (II, III). However, the amount of time actually budgeted for interpersonal safety activities is less than half of that required by company policy (II, III). Analysis of the effectiveness of safety resource utilization is hindered due to a lack of appropriate data (II, V).

Implementation. Personal contacts are emphasized as a means of increasing safety visibility and improving safety consciousness (II, IV). The factory safety committees appear to be effective in communicating management's safety concerns and in improving safety consciousness of committee members (II). It appears, however, that communication of management concern and improved safety attitudes are confined to committee members (II, IV). Emphasis in the meetings has been on complaining rather than on training to spread concern with safety (II, IV). Analysis of records and accident statistics indicates that departmental safety meetings can be most effective in reducing injuries (II, IV). However, the reporting of such meetings is, on the whole, inadequate (II, IV). In addition, the quality and frequency of these meetings vary greatly from department to department (II, IV). The reporting system focuses on L.T.A. reduction information and American National Standards Institute (ANSI) statistics (I, III). L.T.A. reduction is perceived operationally as *the* measure of safety effectiveness (II, III). Safety training of personnel is lacking (III). Analysis of accident reports indicates that training improvements are needed for safety performance of hourly employees (III). Supervisors are thought to be properly trained through experience as hourly employees; however, evidence of this expertise is lacking (II, III).

Outputs. OSHA compliance at the factory was achieved for 1973 with the exception of one citation for noise (II). L.T.A. reduction at the factory from a 1972 figure of 21 to a goal of ten was substantially achieved with a final 1973 figure of 10.51. For the company as a whole, the goal was exceeded, dropping from 15.02 to 7.78 (II). Employee safety consciousness appeared not to have improved, except among safety committee members (II). Except for our presence, no provision exists for the measurement of such safety consciousness (II). Common management assumptions lack support in the present analysis (II, III). L.T.A. reduction apparently did not result from improvements in worker safety attitude (II, III). L.T.A. reduction did not result in reduction in medical or insurance costs (II).

Recommendations

The significance of the L.T.A. reduction goal should be reevaluated (IV). Focus on L.T.A. can lead to conflicts with other goals (III). L.T.A. rate is subject to reporting bias (III). Increased attention to severity rates appears warranted (II).

OSHA standards are a more accurate gauge of safety performance than ANSI standards and should be more closely scrutinized by management (III, IV).

Management concern for safety must be better communicated throughout the plant (III, IV). Position of safety performance in overall performance rating of personnel should be specifically stated (II, III, IV). Such concern is essential for the effective implementation of the Loss Prevention Program (L.P.P.) (IV). Improved communication can help to convey the concept of safety as a goal along with production, rather than safety as a constraint on production (II, III).

Analysis and utilization of personnel time input should receive more attention (III, IV). Improved monitoring of "lost time" budget is warranted (IV). Efforts should be increased to insure that departmental safety meetings are being conducted (II, IV). Time spent at safety committee meetings can be better utilized by increasing emphasis on the training function (IV).

Coordination of factory safety committees and departmental safety meetings is recommended (IV). Training and discussion at factory committee meetings should be coordinated with activities in the departments (II, IV). Factory safety committee members can provide this link (IV). Rotation of committee members should be more frequent than once a year (IV).

Increased emphasis on safety training is advised (III, IV).

The employee's róle in the safety program should be promoted (IV). Involves efforts to relate employee's welfare off the job to his safety on the job (IV). More active use of employee inputs may be expected as safety attitudes improve and as efforts are made to improve those attitudes (II, IV).

Monitoring of employee safety attitudes is needed. Safety committees can provide a proper vehicle for this monitoring (IV).

L.P.P. implementation should focus upon problem areas identified in this report (IV).

The actions recommended in this report can be accomplished within the existing cost structure of the safety program (IV).

II: Approach and Findings

This examination originated with interviews with headquarters management and then focused directly on the operation of the safety program at the company's local factory. While the report refers to a process audit of the "safety program," a more technically correct title would refer to the "safety operations," because at the time of the study, a coordinated, company-wide Loss Prevention Program was still in final developmental stages. The company safety program consisted of a variety of safety-related functions in the various company plants, with many practices and activities being unique to a given factory. The term "safety program" as used in this report refers to those functions, activities, and procedures that had been developed to deal with the prevention of accidents at one factory.

Several distinct elements affecting the safety process were analyzed. In this section, individual attention will be given to each of these elements. The next section will then analyze the relationship of these elements to one another.

Historical Perspective

Headquarters management presently accords safety a position of priority status, although it had never been relegated to a position of low importance in the company. At about the same time as the passage of the Occupational Safety and Health Act of 1970 (OSHA), safety achieved its present status. Headquarters management expressed the general opinion that OSHA did have an effect on the increased attention presently given to safety. However, OSHA is not presented as the cause for management's concerns. Rather, the appearance of the OSHA legislation indicated that safety should no longer rely heavily on the common sense of the worker but rather required positive management action.

Rationale for the Program

The need to maintain safe operations consistent with the law was stated by headquarters management as only a minor justification for the safety program. Rather, the rationale for a strong safety effort was related more closely to both economic and moral concerns.

Economically speaking, an effective safety program can enhance profitability by helping to minimize shut-down time due to accidents on the production line and by decreasing the number of insurance dollars required to compensate employees who are injured and unable to work. Fewer accidents could also favorably affect company medical costs. Carryovers alluding to completed work plans, customer satisfaction, and favorable public opinion were also thought of as enhancing profitability.

The moral rationale deals with a humane concern for the personal safety of employees. This concern was said to be at least as great as that of the economic incentives for safe operations.

Goals of the Program

Approach of Audit. The entire area of the goals of the safety program was examined, from the process of goal setting to the dissemination, acceptance, and interpretation of these goals throughout the company. Accordingly, attention was focused upon these categories of goals:

Identification
Internal Versus External Nature of Goals
Operationalization of Goals
Employee Goals

Findings Related to Goals—Headquarters Management. Goal Setting: The personal safety of employees was said by the company president to rank with production, quality, and sales as a primary consideration. The goal-setting process involves headquarters management and the factory managers from the various operations throughout the country. In consultation, they set goals for specific target levels of performance in safety, productivity, quality, and profit. Headquarters management asserted that the inclusion of safety as a criterion for evaluation of divisional operations is strong evidence of the priority status accorded to safety.

An idealized goal for the safety program as a whole was stated by management to be the achievement of an accident-free environment for personnel. While this goal was pointed to as an ideal, other more operational goals were identified.

Identification of Operational Goals: The first of the operational goals is compliance with the provisions and standards of OSHA, centering primarily on the ability of the company to pass OSHA inspection procedures without citations for violation.

The second operational goal is the achievement of reductions in the company-wide lost-time-accident (LTA) frequency rate. The LTA rate indicates the number of reported accidents resulting in worker lost time per million person-hours of activity. For 197_ a target goal for the company was set at an LTA of ____, a figure representing a reduction from the company's previous year's average.

Headquarters management stressed the goal of LTA reduction to a much greater extent than the goal of OSHA compliance. OSHA compliance was viewed as a fact of life, a necessary response to federal legislation, but was not seen in itself as any guarantee of safer operations. The operationalization of a company-wide safety effort appears to have been very much geared to the goal of LTA reduction.

The third operational goal was that of developing a proper safety attitude on the part of personnel, which entails the establishment of an employee consciousness of the importance of safety considerations as part of the everyday routine. Some of the headquarters managers viewed the front-line supervisor as the key individual in fostering the development of safety attitudes. Others felt that efforts to increase personal safety concern should be focused directly on the hourly workers, the aim being to instill in the worker a concern for safety so that he or she becomes a safe person and displays a social concern for the safety of others.

It should be noted that the development of safety consciousness is not easily defined in measurable terms. Thus, while this goal was accepted, it did not have the same operational measure of success as the other two goals. Its measurement is discussed in the section on Outputs.

Internal Versus External Nature of Goals: The external stimulus provided by the OSHA regulations has been mentioned, but this government-legal stimulus has not been the only external concern. The company has also attempted to maintain a favorable safety record in comparison with its competitors in the same industry.

Three other external forces may also have strong interests in the safety effort—the National Safety Council, the company's insurance company, and the labor unions that represent company employees. The National Safety Council, as a monitoring agency for safety operations of industry in general, must be aware of the safety performance of the company. The insurance company stands to benefit from accident reductions through lower compensation outlays and a corresponding reduction of the record-keeping costs related to such claims. The labor unions have a vested interest in the safety and welfare of their members. However, despite the apparent concern of these groups, their impact on the goals of the company appears to be minimal. Headquarters management included none of these entities as significant factors affecting the goal-setting process of the safety problem.

Findings Related to Goals—Plant Level. The discussion to this point has dealt with the goals of the program as perceived by a sample of headquarters management. Additional data provided by personnel at the local factory indicate that such perceptions are not universally understood throughout the company.

Identification of Goals—Middle Management and Supervisors: Middle-management and supervisory personnel at the plant expressed an awareness of top management's stated humane concern for employees. However, these individuals asserted that higher management had a much greater interest in the safety program as a means of reducing costs and avoiding unfavorable publicity. The increased safety activity was largely attributed to the necessity for OSHA compliance.

OSHA compliance, therefore, was perceived to be a high-priority concern of top management. This priority was equated not with management's concern for employees but rather with its desire to avoid unfavorable publicity and possible legal action.

LTA rate reduction was also well understood as a desired goal of top management. In fact, from an operational standpoint, middle managers and supervisors spoke almost solely in terms of LTA reduction as a desired output.

Employee safety attitude was a subject of some disagreement among middle managers and supervisors. Some believed that employee safety goals were confined only to the worker's desire to remain unharmed. Consequently, workers would commit unsafe acts so long as they were reasonably sure of avoiding an accident or had been able to get away with such an act in the past. These workers had to be coerced to follow safety procedures. Other managers and supervisors, however, believed that workers were safety conscious or could easily become so. They felt that employees were well aware of management's efforts to provide an active safety program.

The safety-attitude goal was not accepted by all supervisors and managers as an important goal. While some viewed it as an important means of attaining an effective safety program, others thought that supervisors must act as policemen to enforce safety practices.

Internal Versus External Nature of Goals—Management and Employee Perceptions: Hourly employees recognized an increase in management's attention to safety. This emphasis was attributed to management's desire to save money and to avoid OSHA citations. OSHA was widely identified by hourly employees as the major reason for management's concern for safety.

Plant personnel identified the labor union as a potentially important influence on the company's safety goals, but the general opinion was that the union had not, so far, expressed much of an interest in attempting to affect the goal-setting process of the safety program.

Employee Goals: In general, the employees viewed their own safety goal as a desire to avoid injury on the job, but they asserted that the importance of safety as an employee goal was constrained by several factors. Some stated that their own personal concern for safety was blunted by the recognition that supervisors engaged in unsafe practices. Others said that the impulse to stop work because of a marginally unsafe condition was blunted by their perception that production was of primary importance. Still others had no real safety goal as a part of their job performance.

Perhaps somewhat surprisingly, several of the hourly workers were not even aware of the existence of a safety program (see the discussion of the Factory Safety Committee in the section on implementation of the program). Of those employees who were aware of the safety efforts of management, the expressed goal of reducing the LTA was widely identified.

Goals at the Plant Level: OSHA and the presumed dollar benefits to the company were recognized at all levels of the plant as stimuli to the safety effort of management. Similarly, the LTA reduction goal was widely perceived throughout the factory. However, it appears that neither the safety attitude goal nor the importance of safety as a management goal has been well communicated or accepted throughout the plant.

Inputs to the Safety Program

Approach of Audit. In order to accomplish the identified goals of the safety program, various resources must be utilized. In this section, the nature and origin of such resources are identified. Inputs are examined according to four classes:

> Company Resources
> Noncompany Resources
> Employee Resources
> Social Costs

Findings Related to Inputs. Company Resources: Certain company resources are immediately recognizable in dollar amounts—for example, dollars expended for repairs and maintenance relating to OSHA compliance. Other inputs, such as employee time utilized in safety meetings, can be calculated in dollar amounts by multiplying the employee hours devoted to such activities by the wage rate for these employees. Other company resource inputs are less easy to qualify. For example, the company pays for a number of items of safety equipment, but certain items are accounted for as part of the original employee clothing issue while others are clearly identified as safety expenditures.

Several types of inputs can be directly identified with OSHA. In terms of dollar value, the most important OSHA-related expenditures are those for repair and maintenance of facilities. Figures provided for operations at the plant show this amount to be approximately $____ per month.

Time spent by employees on safety activities has also become an important company resource, especially since interpersonal contact between individuals at all levels of the company was stressed as a crucial means of achieving increased safety consciousness.

The dollar value of time spent on safety can be traced to the personnel involved in these activities. In certain cases, individuals are specifically employed for the safety function, while others have numerous other responsibilities in addition to safety. The latter would include supervisory personnel and employees assigned to the factory safety committees. Specific dollar costs for salaries were not available to the audit team but can be easily obtained from corporate records.

In certain instances, the identification of time spent on safety is more difficult to discern. Time spent by employees at factory safety committee or departmental safety meetings is noted on punch cards and recorded as part of a factory "lost-time" budget classification. However, in the case of supervisors or maintenance employees, it is not always possible to state that an activity is exclusively safety related. Activities to ensure the safe condition of a given area may appear, for example, to be as easily chargeable to general housekeeping as to safety.

Calculations can be made of the dollar value of the time inputs for specific safety activities. The primary activities in the plant are the factory safety committee and the departmental safety meetings. Salaries of management personnel participating in such meetings for a certain number of hours per month can be calculated.

Additional company resource inputs to safety should also be mentioned. The company provides the majority of the safety gear required for its employees. However, an accurate accounting of these costs could not be ascertained by the audit team. Company personnel explained that such figures were not available because certain of the amounts were grouped in broad accounting classifications and thus the safety component of that classification could not be accurately identified.

Other expenditures relate to safety signs and reminders placed strategically throughout the factory and to medical costs involving accidents. Again, however, specific amounts were not available. For the present time, such input classes can only be identified and must await future efforts for a more accurate accounting of actual amounts expended.

Noncompany resources: Noncompany resources were identified as coming principally from two sources, the regional Safety Council and the insurance company. In one sense, these resources are also "company resources" in that the company pays for the services of these two concerns. Unfortunately, specific cost figures for these services were not available.

The Safety Council can play an active role in providing statistics on the performance of other enterprises, in the availability of expertise and possible safety training aids for company adoption, in providing updates on federal safety and health standards and requirements, and in the availability of a safety magazine.

The insurance carrier for the plant has a direct concern about the amount of compensable losses resulting from accidents. The company's loss prevention staff has been utilized for consultative purposes. Required plant inspections by the insurance company can also be utilized as an aid in identifying problem areas in the factory.

Another potential noncompany resource is the labor union, although it has not yet been actively involved in the company safety effort. Safety appears to be very much a bargaining item in labor-management relations. Thus, cooperative efforts between union and management to combat safety problems have been absent. But despite the problems surrounding the need for bargaining between labor and management, it appears that more positive use could be made of the union as a safety resource (see Recommendations).

Employee Resources: Employee resources primarily involve amounts paid by the workers for protective gear. The company provides most of this equipment so that employee out-of-pocket costs are comparatively minor. The personal time of the employee has not been considered to any great extent in the program because time spent by the worker on safety committees is compensated by the company. (However, the audit team is aware of at least one committee member who has attended factory safety committee meetings on his own time, even though he was scheduled to work another shift.)

Social Costs: Social costs refers to those costs incurred by segments of society as a result of the implementation of the safety program. While hard data are lacking, it does seem possible to identify a potential social cost associated with the safety program.

One form of social cost, although in this case perhaps only a hypothetical one, would come about if the production lines were to be shut down at every indication that an accident might possibly happen. When production is shut down because of an accident or because of a large probability of such an event, this is clearly a cost to the company (a company resource input). If, though, the practice became that of a production shut-down at even the slightest indication of an unsafe condition, the cost could be carried over to society. The losses of productivity could result in a reduction of the work force and would also adversely affect earnings. In turn, such a policy would be detrimental to the stockholders of the firm and would harm wholesalers, retailers, and consumers who depend upon the availability of the product. In such a case, the loss of employment to certain individuals would be the cost of ensuring that the remainder of the work force remained as nearly accident-free as possible. This discussion takes matters to the extreme and is hypothetical, but it is important to note that such a trade-off might exist. Such an analysis may be particularly important for other types of social programs.

Summary and Discussion. Several resource inputs to the safety program have been identified, some external, but for the most part from within the company.

At the local plant, OSHA-related expenditures were found to be approximately $____ per month. The dollar value of employee time inputs to the safety program is presently budgeted at $____ per month. Additional company resources were identified, but accurate information on the amounts expended for these items was not provided to the audit team.

That such data could not be made available is significant. Headquarters management has firmly asserted that safety is a priority management concern. Yet as this discussion indicates, the nature and amounts of expenditures to pursue this concern are scattered about in several accounts rather than contained in a safety budget classification. Unfortunately, the fact that such data are not presently collected in a uniform manner makes difficult any attempt to determine whether resources are being utilized optimally. Thus, efforts to determine an optimal mix of such inputs would require the adequate collection of actual figures (see section on Analysis of Program Processes and Recommendations, below).

Implementation of the Safety Program

Implementation of the safety program was approached according to three factors:

The organizational environment and structure in which the safety program has operated;
Communications and feedback mechanisms provided for the safety program;
Analysis of specific procedures that have been implemented.

Organizational Environment. As discussed earlier, headquarters management has asserted that safety is one of its major concerns, and safety is now said to be an important criterion in the evaluation of the performance of factory managers. In addition, headquarters management stated that the factory managers recognized a competitive aspect to safety. Performance at individual facilities is made known to the other factories through widespread use of comparative accident statistics. Headquarters management also said that workers in the plants took pride in their safety records and were rewarded for successful efforts through publicity in the company newspaper.

While the importance of safety to performance evaluation may well be recognized by factory managers, there is reason to question such recognition by lower-level factory personnel. Analysis of safety operations in one factory indicates that managers and supervisors below the plant manager level are uncertain about how safety performance affects an individual's overall performance rating and how they should relate the newly perceived emphasis on safety to their own actions. Lacking clear guidelines, individual managers and supervisors were guided in their approach to safety by their knowledge of the approaches taken by their superiors. Thus, safety at the plant level appeared to be viewed more as a part of an informal performance measure than as part of a formal evaluative mechanism. While policy discussions between the department head and supervisors were carried out in a few departments, for the most part neither training nor formal guidelines were offered to supervisors throughout the plant to aid them in confronting unsafe conditions of a minor sort while being pressed to meet production schedules.

Organization Structure. The safety operations of the company receive the full-time attention of the Safety manager, whose position was created in 1971, subsequent to the passage of OSHA. Among his many duties is the responsibility for maintaining an awareness of the most current OSHA provisions and for monitoring company-wide activities relating to OSHA. He is also responsible for compiling and communicating safety statistics for all of the company's facilities and for coordinating company safety policy from plant to plant. Much of his time and effort has been devoted to the development of the Loss Prevention Program, which is intended to lead to a more uniform, company-wide safety policy. Despite the title, the Safety manager serves a staff function and has no line authority.

At one plant level, responsibility for the safety function has generally been placed in the hands of the Personnel manager. An exception to this is the local factory, where there is also a safety department head who reports to the personnel manager. The department head's duties correspond to those of the company Safety manager, but they are limited to this plant. Because of their proximity, the Safety manager and the plant Safety Department head have worked quite closely together. The filling of these two positions in 1971 was said by personnel in the factory to have given safety a "shot in the arm" at the local plant.

Communications and Feedback. It was mentioned above that plant-level supervisors are guided in their actions by recognition of the safety concerns of their superiors. Knowledge of a superior's concern also appears to have played an important role company-wide in the area of safety communications and feedback. In one region in particular, the regional manager demonstrates his concern for safety by frequent personal contacts with his subordinates. Divisional managers in this region must immediately contact the regional manager by phone in the event of a disabling accident at the plant level. The personal concern displayed by the regional manager and the response by the plant managers has contributed to improved safety performance and is often pointed to by headquarters management as an example of effective policy. However, it must be stated again that an effective safety program should not rely upon the personal concern of individual managers, because this can lead to very irregular patterns of communication and feedback and consequently to undesirable safety performance.

Communication between headquarters and the plant is less of a problem for the local factory because of close proximity, but attention can be focused upon the means of communication and feedback regarding safety within the plant.

The hub of the factory safety communications network is the safety department head. In monitoring the safety operations within the plant, he records reported accidents, prepares accident reports, and coordinates the plant safety activities.

Communication of safety concerns is attempted through both direct and indirect means. Indirect communication is through the widespread use of safety signs and slogans. More direct means of safety communication are the factory safety committees and the departmental safety meetings, but before discussing these activities, the plant's extensive accident reporting system will be discussed.

Accident Reporting System: The reporting and recording of accidents is a major task. Statistics are presently tabulated according to two sets of standards. The company LTA goal is based upon safety standards developed by the American National Standards Institute (ANSI). OSHA record-keeping procedures require that accidents be recorded and classified according to different criteria. Specific OSHA forms must be used and the information supplied upon request to the government. (Problems created by the use of two accident reporting standards are discussed in Part Two of Section III, Analysis of Program Process.) The safety department head is responsible for the preparation of accident reports within the plant.

Accident statistics reported plant-wide are those calculated according to ANSI standards. Disabling injuries as defined by these standards require the preparation of an accident report by the immediate supervisor and the attention of an Accident Investigation Committee. The details of the accident are discussed at the factory safety committee meetings, and the report of the investigating team is distributed to the factory manager, managers throughout the plant, and the safety committee members.

Accidents that do not require lost time are classified as "serious" if medical treatment is required. An injured worker reports to the medical office for treatment. Supervisors are responsible for reporting such accidents, and the medical staff provides a report of treatments to the safety department head.

Accident statistics for all departments are tabulated by the Safety Department head, and a comparative departmental standing based on safety performance is calculated. However, unlike the earlier identified safety competition among factories, little emphasis has been placed within this factory upon safety as a competitive element among departments.

Factory Safety Committees: Two safety committee meetings are conducted each month in the factory. One of these, the factory safety committee meeting, consists only of hourly workers who meet once each month. These employees are chosen by management to represent the various departments within the plant. The second committee, the Joint Labor-Management Safety Committee, meets two weeks earlier and consists of certain members of the first committee along with supervisory personnel. Both of these meetings are conducted by a member of the management staff (who serves as monthly chairperson on a rotating basis), with the safety department head in attendance. Each meeting lasts approximately one hour.

At the Factory Safety Committee meeting, hourly employees are given the opportunity to identify any safety-related problems that have occurred in their areas. Suggestions are requested as to how safety can be better achieved. The Joint Labor-Management Safety Committee meeting is then very much a progress report in which supervisory personnel explain to the chairperson and hourly worker representatives their actions or inactions regarding suggestions made at the first meeting. A portion of both of these meetings is devoted to a report by the safety department head of the most current accident statistics for the plant.

Departmental Safety Meetings: Safety meetings in the departments are designed to communicate the message of safety to the workers in the areas where they actually work. These meetings, of 15 minutes' duration, are designed to be discussions that focus on safety matters directly pertinent to individual departments.

While these meetings are supposed to be held on a biweekly basis, there is apparently little control exerted by management, and it was not an uncommon practice for a supervisor not to hold the meeting. The reasons for not holding meetings seem to be related either to a supervisor's own lack of concern about such meetings or to his desire to maintain continuity of productive output. In any case, neither company nor plant procedures exercised sufficient control to ensure that these meetings were held. This is significant because the analysis that follows indicates that the departmental meetings can be an important means of accident prevention.

Analysis of Specific Safety Procedures. The discussion that follows examines the safety activities as they were observed to operate in the plant. Analysis is focused upon the factory safety committees and the department safety meetings. Section III, the Analysis of Program Processes, extends this analysis and examines an alternative use of accident and safety-related statistics.

Factory Safety Committees: A number of important findings can be related to the factory safety committees. The committees appear to have been a positive factor in increasing the concern of the committee members for safety matters. The communications channel provided by the safety committees can improve the visibility of management's safety concern. However, this channel, if improperly utilized, could result in exactly the opposite effect. If suggestions or complaints of the workers receive little management attention, then the professed concern of management for the personal safety of employees could be discounted by the workers.

Another important finding concerning the safety committees relates to the activities at these meetings. At present, the meetings are used exclusively for discussing safety suggestions and complaints. No provision is made for using the time for safety training. However, it was indicated that in previous years attempts were made to train committee members under a somewhat different committee framework. That experience reportedly led to a situation in which the committee members received the training benefits but did not pass them on to the workers in the department. Consequently, training activities were removed from the committee framework when it was revised.

At present, therefore, committee members serve as safety representatives for the departments only to the extent that complaints and suggestions can be channeled through them to management. No formal attempt has been made to coordinate the activities of the member at the committee meetings with his or her actions back in the department, either through involvement in the departmental meetings or through possible training efforts with coworkers. Specific suggestions for utilizing the time and efforts of safety committee members are detailed in the Recommendations section.

Departmental Safety Meetings: As stated, these meetings are to occur on a biweekly basis. Reports of the meetings are written up by the departmental supervisor and channeled to the Safety Department head. As already noted, the format of the meetings has not been uniform, nor have they been held consistently in all departments.

An attempt was made to determine the effectiveness of these meetings. While a logical assumption may well be that the occurrence of such meetings will help to cut the frequency of accidents, any analysis that could verify such a view has been lacking.

An examination was made of the departmental safety meeting reports and the supervisor's reports of accidents in the factory. The attempt was made to determine whether there was any relationship between the holding of departmental meetings and the prevention of accidents.

The analysis indicates that departmental meetings have indeed been important aids in reducing the number of accidents per person-hour. The figures mean that when topics were discussed in the departmental meetings, a significant drop in accidents relating to those topics also occurred.

These findings are quite important. They indicate that departmental meetings can be very beneficial in helping to reduce accidents. The significance of these findings becomes even greater when consideration is given to the previously mentioned fact that the departmental safety meetings are not at present being regularly conducted in all departments. Analysis of the reports was made more difficult by the fact that reports of departmental meetings did not appear to be submitted to the Safety Department head on any uniform basis. This absence of reports points to the tentative nature of the findings of the analysis of report forms in a statistical sense.

However, these problems appear to have even more important implications for the effective communication and feedback of safety matters. The departmental Safety manager has little, if any, way of knowing whether his safety meetings are helping to prevent accidents. The report that he fills out merely communicates that certain safety-related topics have been discussed. Without feedback about the effectiveness of such discussions, the filing of these reports may well be viewed by the supervisor as bothersome or meaningless. At the same time, despite his efforts, the Safety Department head is unable to provide such feedback for the reasons just stated: The information requirements of the two report forms do not permit an adequate assessment of departmental meeting effectiveness, and he is further hampered by the absence of reports from some departments.

The present analysis should, therefore, enable the Safety Department head to provide necessary feedback about the effectiveness of the meetings. And, equally importantly, the findings suggest that efforts should be directed toward improving the frequency and reporting of departmental safety meetings. (This point will be examined more fully in the Recommendations section.)

A similar analysis was made of the accident report forms in an effort to identify the types and causes of accidents reported in the departments. This analysis is discussed in Section III, Analysis of Program Processes.

Outputs of the Safety Program. Outputs of the safety program can be directly related to and compared with the goals of the program, although, in some instances, the association between goal and output is less easily identifiable than in others.

OSHA Compliance: OSHA compliance involves the ability to meet all OSHA standards and to pass an OSHA inspection without citation. Achievement of this goal can be noted through the correction of deficiencies in the absence of a formal inspection or as the outcome of an inspection by an OSHA compliance officer. For the plant involved, a formal OSHA inspection did take place, and the company received just one citation, for noise, a problem that has confronted industry in general. Thus, with this one exception, the goal of OSHA compliance was met.

LTA Reduction: The company was significantly successful in reducing the LTA rate. The actual company-wide reduction was even greater than the figure set in the goal, and a comparison of the company with industry performance for the past four years indicates the company's improved LTA position. There was also a significant improvement in the LTA rate at the local plant.

Safety Attitude Goal: There is little statistical information available on whether or not personnel have become more concerned about safety matters.

Headquarters management assumed that achievement of this goal would be reflected in an overall improvement in safety effectiveness, particularly through an improved LTA. However, this assumption of improved LTA performance is the only indicator of the success of the program in achieving greater safety consciousness.

Interviews conducted at all levels of management indicate a further assumption that increased safety consciousness by workers would be attained as a result of a highly viable safety effort by management. Discussions with the hourly employees, however, indicated that safety awareness or consciousness was more likely to result from an individual's inclusion on the plant safety committee. Improvements in safety attitude have apparently not been uniform throughout the plant, and there is at present no way (except for the interviews of the audit team) to indicate the extent to which the safety attitude goal has been accomplished.

Analysis: It is obvious that the company did many things right in its safety effort. Very significant is the fact that the most talked-about goal—LTA reduction—was not only met but exceeded.

However, perhaps equally important is the indication that certain intuitively appealing notions regarding safety effectiveness have been left unsupported. The lack of support for the contended relationship between LTA reduction and safety consciousness is important to note. Additionally, appealing notions relating to cost reductions have lacked verification in the present analysis. As many of the cost data for the program were unavailable and in some cases unknown, a detailed analysis of the cost effectiveness of the program was not possible.

Nevertheless, there are several indications that the effectiveness of the safety program—as measured by OSHA compliance and a significant LTA reduction—did not lead to overall improvements in costs in such areas as medical and insurance outlays.

Section III identifies several reasons why the LTA rate may not provide a true indication of the effectiveness of the safety program. In the meantime, a brief look at the severity rate performance of the company can give an indication of why the costs did not significantly decrease. While the LTA was almost half that of the previous year, the severity rate actually increased. Briefly stated, this rate indicates that equivalent working days lost due to accidents increased per million person-hours worked despite the decrease in reported disabling injuries. The extent of compensable claims is directly related to the number of lost work days and is, therefore, an indication of why compensation costs did not decrease. While comparatively fewer disabling injuries were reported, those that did occur required a correspondingly greater amount of compensable work time.

This discussion should not be construed to mean that the company concern for safety has not been worth the effort. Rather it is meant to indicate that additional efforts are needed to gauge accurately the effectiveness of the safety program. At present, several intuitively appealing notions are used to support the safety effort, and the effectiveness of that effort is largely measured according to LTA measurement. The sections that follow will identify several pitfalls regarding LTA as a measure of effectiveness and will identify alternative measures of program performance. Recommendations will be made concerning ways to improve the measurement of the accomplishment of the safety attitude goal.

III: Analysis of Program Processes

Section II presented an analysis of the research findings for individual aspects of the safety program. The present section attempts to indicate how these individual aspects relate to one another throughout the operation of the program. For example, while three operational goals have been identified, analysis is needed of whether the pursuit of one goal facilitates or hinders the pursuit of another. Questions also need to be raised about the utilization of resources and the possible compatibility or conflict of such usage for the achievement of these goals.

This section is divided into two parts. The first examines possible conflicts that might arise in the attempt to achieve company safety goals. In the second part, analysis is focused upon the relationship between the various activities and the problems that have arisen in the implementation of the safety program.

Part One: Goal Conflicts

Safety Goals and the Profit Motive. Safety pays. This is the theme of many of the notices from the office of the headquarters Safety manager. It is, in fact, a common viewpoint among headquarters management that effective safety operations will enhance profit. And this view does indeed have intuitive appeal, for effective safety operations should lead to fewer accidents, thus resulting in reduced numbers of work stoppages, lower insurance dollar payouts, and decreasing medical costs.

Thus, there would appear to be little potential conflict in promoting safety in a profit-making operation. Indeed, it was stated by those concerned with the safety program that safety activities have been promoted to higher management on the basis of this theme of profit enhancement and on the grounds of management's traditional concern for employee welfare.

However, the question of safety compatibility or conflict with profit performance remains unresolved. It was pointed out earlier that accidents could be eliminated entirely if production never occurred, a condition clearly in conflict with the profit incentive. It was also pointed out, however, by the medical director, that an effective safety program under normal conditions of production may do little to reduce medical costs and thereby enhance profits. Often no fine line could be drawn between medical treatments specifically related to safety and those for ailments resulting from off-the-job activities.

Therefore, the safety program's contribution to profit has never been clearly established. While management can point to studies of other firms that indicate the profitability of safety effectiveness, the present safety reporting system cannot adequately provide such verification for this company.

For the present discussion, the implications of the uncertainty of safety effectiveness and profit enhancement are twofold. First, it must be recognized that acceptance of the profit enhancement motive is not based on facts directly derived from the company's experience. Acceptance is based upon the experience of others and upon some appealing suppositions. Employees in general stated that management safety activities were a result of profit incentives and the desire to remain free of OSHA penalties. Managerial concern for the worker is very much overlooked by employees. Consequently, management's efforts may presently be directed toward profit enhancement motives that are not realizable but yet whose presence overshadows another important management concern, that of the welfare of the employees.

It should be recognized that a very inefficient safety program would detract from the firm's profit picture because of the inefficiencies and costs created by an excessive number of accidents. However, at present, there is little way of knowing at exactly what level safety operations are efficient in an economic sense for the company. As will be discussed in the section on Recommendations, part of the reason for this appears to be that economic inputs to the safety program are not as rigorously classified or identified as would be necessary for such a calculation. Another reason appears to be related to the measure of effectiveness most often applied to safety in this company—LTA rates, discussed in Part Two of this section.

OSHA Compliance and Reduced LTA. OSHA regulations specifically address the issue of providing safe facilities. But while safe facilities are an important part of any efficient accident prevention program, it has been contended by those directly concerned with the safety program that the specific requirements of OSHA can, in some cases, present the most efficient allocation of safety resources. Another possible conflict between these two goals results from the recording requirements of each. OSHA record-keeping requirements classify accidents quite differently from the method the company utilizes to measure LTA. These differences can lead to some very real conflicts between the necessities of adequate accident reporting and the utilization of these reports. These differences and conflicts will be discussed in detail below.

OSHA Compliance and Increased Safety Awareness: There appears to be a good deal of harmony in the attempts to achieve these two goals. Already noted was the fact that subordinates' attitudes toward safety have often been guided by perception of the superior's concern. Thus, the commitment of management to the maintenance of safe facilities could contribute substantially to the credibility of the organization's concern for safety. However, the very nature of this credibility could lead to conflict.

The fact that much of management's concern for safety has been evidenced since the passage of OSHA has led to a degree of cynicism on the part of some lower-level management and hourly workers. Consequently, awareness has been heightened, but it is a perceived awareness of management's regard for the law rather than its concern for employee welfare.

Another conflict could arise as a result of successful efforts to improve employee safety awareness. Several managers stated that OSHA could prove to be dangerous to the firm because its provisions gave the hourly employee a potentially more active voice regarding working conditions. Increased safety awareness could lead to the exercise of this potential through the request for an OSHA inspection. Frequent inspections increase the chances of receiving citations and require the time of certain company personnel. It appears, therefore, that attempts to create safety awareness must be followed as well by action to ensure that management is meeting the rising expectations of its more safety-conscious work force.

Reduced LTA and Increased Safety Awareness: Several common elements characterize the attempts to achieve these goals. Headquarters management stated, for example, that one of the best ways to reduce the number of accidents was through the attitude-change approach. Thus, there was extensive use of signs, personal contacts with workers, and an attempt to involve people directly with the safety program through safety committee and departmental safety meeting participation. In addition, there was an assumption that changes in safety awareness would be reflected in the reported LTA index. This latter assumption is crucial to the safety program as it currently operates, but there are indications that such an assumption may not be valid.

According to statements contained in the company's Loss Prevention Program, a study has indicated that for every on-the-job injury reported, hourly employees could recall at least three injuries that were not reported. It is likely, therefore, that an increased safety awareness could result in a greater inclination on the part of employees to report these accidents.

On the other hand, supervisors are presently becoming aware of the need to keep reported accidents at a low level in order to enhance their performance ratings. Clearly, if this happens, a definite conflict arises between an employee's desire to express his concern by reporting accidents and his recognition that his immediate supervisor views such actions unfavorably.

The LTA is perhaps less susceptible to reporting biases in that it relates to actual disabling or lost-time injuries. However, the same type of pressure might be exerted in marginal cases. The point to be recognized is that the goal of safety concern, as operationalized by the employee through the reporting of accidents, can be in direct conflict with the goal of a lower reported LTA. Such a conflict can create problems both for proper accident reporting and prevention and for interpersonal relationships between employees and supervisors.

The assumed correlation between improved attitude and LTA reduction cannot, therefore, be readily accepted. Presently, however, there is no ongoing system to measure the achievement of the attitude goal. The importance of the relationship between these goals should not be overlooked. As will be discussed in the Recommendations section, methods should be developed to measure the accomplishment of both more adequately.

Part Two: Program Analysis

Several problems, both present and potential, have been identified up to this point. Part Two of this section attempts to identify the reasons for these problems through an examination of the manner in which the activities associated with the safety program relate to one another.

Problems with Goal Communication. In the Approach and Findings section, it was reported that plant-level personnel attributed much of the perceived management concern for safety to the profit motive and the presence of OSHA. As was noted, this contrasts with headquarters management assertions that an equally important factor is their humane concern for all employees.

Deterrents to an effective safety program have arisen because of the misperceptions. For example, a supervisor who is not convinced of the importance of safety either to his superiors or to his own performance rating will be less likely to halt production for marginal safety reasons than will one who correctly perceives safety as an important performance criterion. A similar comparison can be made between a supervisor who recognizes the importance of safety and one who recognizes only the effect of safety on profitability and productivity. Thus, it is imperative that management make explicit its concern and operationalize precise safety guidelines for supervisors and hourly workers to follow.

Similar problems can be created when any one of the three operational goals is emphasized to the neglect of others. The danger of overemphasis is most evident with the LTA reduction goal. As stated in the previous section, plant personnel most widely identified the LTA reduction goal as the primary measure of safety effectiveness. Consequently, the majority of those who did recognize safety as an important concern viewed the LTA goal as their most important criterion of performance.

Problems with Resource Utilization. Expenditures for safe facilities were identified as the major resource requirement for OSHA compliance. However, LTA reduction and employee safety consciousness also require such expenditures to a certain extent: Much emphasis is placed on using the time of hourly and managerial employees for specific safety-related activities. It is obvious, therefore, that the expenditure of large sums of money to provide the safety of facilities will not in itself lead to the accomplishment of the other two goals.

It was noted in the Inputs section that OSHA-related expenditures for repair and maintenance were more than double the amount required for employee or personnel time inputs. This comparison does not include the salary of the factory Safety Department head nor any proration of salary for possible contacts with plants made by the company safety manager. However, these salary figures would not relate more to the other two goals than to OSHA. In fact, the monitoring of OSHA provisions is a primary responsibility of both individuals. Therefore, even excluding these salary figures in the comparison, OSHA-related expenditures far exceed those required to pursue specifically the other two goals.

This is not to say that, because there are three safety goals, there should be equal amounts of money spent on each. However, because the employee time input is so important to both LTA reduction and employee safety consciousness, the magnitude of resources utilized for OSHA becomes even more significant. Furthermore, the amounts actually budgeted for employee safety time are far less than would be needed if all allowable departmental safety meetings were actually held.

Consequently, it appears that the personnel time input is being under-utilized in the safety program, although a word of caution is in order. The mere spending of time does not necessarily guarantee effectiveness in achieving safety goals. Nevertheless, the fact that personnel time is underutilized seems apparent, as is evidenced by the analysis of available budget figures and by the discussion of departmental safety meetings in the Implementation section.

An additional word is necessary regarding the utilization of personnel time. "Training" is not a part of the formal attempt to achieve any of the safety goals. The concluding part of this section presents an analysis of accident report forms that indicates that safety training is indeed a subject deserving of closer management attention.

Problems with Use of Accident Statistics. As noted earlier, accident statistics are accumulated according to two sets of standards. The company sets its performance goals on ANSI standard statistics and must also classify and report to the government accident statistics based on OSHA guidelines.

The two standards differ both in units of measure and in the classification of accidents. A detailed distinction between these standards can be made by consulting both the American National Standards Institute Standard Z16.1–1967, "Method of Recording and Measuring Work Injury Experience," and a government document entitled *Recordkeeping Requirements Under the Williams-Steiger Occupational Safety and Health Act of 1970*. However, an adequate distinction for purposes of this report can be made by referring to the definitions provided on the company's own form (quoted material that follows is from that form).

The unit of measure for ANSI standards is based upon one million employee-hours of exposure. Thus, the LTA or Disabling Injury Frequency Rate expresses the number of disabling injuries recorded for the equivalent of one million person-hours worked. The OSHA equivalent of this rate, the Incidence Rate, "is the number of recordable injuries and illnesses per 200,000 employee hours worked."

The standards also differ in how accidents are classified. The basic difference between them is this: ANSI standards label an injury as disabling if an employee is not physically able to report to work, whereas the OSHA equivalent classified an injury as recordable if the employee cannot perform his normal duties, even though he is physically able to report for work.

The distinction is significant. As related earlier, a great deal of emphasis was placed on the LTA reduction goals within the factory. Part One of this section indicated that a possible means of lowering the rate would be to exhort the employee to work, although injured, at a less strenuous job. This type of activity would be counted in the OSHA statistic because the fact that the employee transferred to another job requires that the incident be reported.

The ANSI standard, therefore, appears to be much more susceptible to manipulation than does the OSHA, and the latter appears to provide for a more accurate measure of safety effectiveness. It appears, therefore, that the accumulation of statistics as required by OSHA can be more than just another burdensome necessity imposed by government and may instead aid the company in more effectively assessing its safety efforts. The possible use of both ANSI and OSHA statistics will be discussed in the Recommendations section.

Analysis of Accident Reports. The previous sections reported the methods of collection and distribution of accident statistics. The audit team has attempted another use, that of analyzing the information provided on the supervisor accident investigation forms. These reports were examined in an effort to determine which types of accidents occurred most frequently and to identify the primary causes of accidents. The study focused on plant-wide statistics and on those for individual departments.

For the factory as a whole, three major causes of accidents were most frequently cited: (1) dangerous practices (36 percent), (2) inability of the victim (20 percent), and (3) defective equipment (11 percent). The types of accidents occurring were primarily sprains and strains (31 percent), scratches (20 percent), and abrasions and contusions (16 percent). Of all accidents occurring, 17 percent were disabling.

The company-wide statistics and the departmental figures render a significant finding. Almost two-thirds (65 percent) of all accidents were said to be caused by dangerous practices or the inability of the victim. Therefore, a majority of reported accidents occurred either because the individual performed his duties in an unsafe manner or because the individual was unqualified to be performing that given task. This would seem to have important implications for the training function within the plant. For those carrying out dangerous practices, more safety training would seem to be potentially useful. The need for greater management attention to the safety component of accepted practices is also indicated. In addition, training would help alleviate the problems attributed to inability of the victim. Such individuals could either be properly trained to perform the task in a safe manner or at least educated as to the inadvisability of performing the task.

The need for emphasis upon safety training, therefore, seems evident. The accident reports can also be analyzed to identify problems associated with individual departments. For example, inability of the victim was a particular problem for two specific departments and was quite frequently cited in some other departments as well. Also, while training is apparently a factory-wide need, certain accident causes are more closely associated with one department than another.

Analysis of the reports in this manner can aid in the preparation of an effective accident prevention strategy. The figures indicate the importance of safety training to a company-wide safety strategy and also point to the need to devise specific approaches suited to the individual problems of departments. A strategy utilizing the training element could positively affect the recorded accident rate and should improve employee safety attitudes, especially since dangerous practices were so often noted as accident causes.

IV: Recommendations

> *The significance of the LTA reduction goal for management purposes should be reevaluated.*
>
> - Increased emphasis should be placed on injury severity rates.
> - Safety performance should not be equated primarily with LTA reduction.
> - Effective communication is required to convey the concept of safety as a goal.

While OSHA compliance, LTA reduction, and improved employee safety consciousness were identified as operational subgoals by headquarters management, the goal of LTA reduction received primary attention at the plant. Supervisors apparently equated LTA reduction with safety performance and perceived that they would be evaluated, if at all, on the basis of LTA performance.

It was pointed out in the Analysis of Process section that the statistics relating to LTA can be vulnerable to reporting biases. Furthermore, it was demonstrated that successful efforts to improve employee safety consciousness—as expressed in one manner through the reporting of accidents or unsafe acts and conditions—could lead to conflicts with supervisors who feel that they must keep the reported LTA at a minimum.

Additionally, the data as presently accumulated do not lend support to the contention that LTA reduction would save the company money through lower dollar insurance compensation outlays. A possible explanation is that while frequencies were improved, the severity of those accidents that were reported was correspondingly greater. Investigation of the causes and circumstances of severe accidents and vigorous efforts to correct noted problems appear to be essential.

This discussion should not be taken to mean that the achievement of the LTA goal was unimportant. The fact that the LTA was drastically reduced is a strong indication that safety goals can be met. Efforts were marshaled in a dramatic way, from many directions within the firm, to achieve this goal. The point to be made is that from a practical point of view, concentration on the LTA can be both dysfunctional and unrewarding as explained earlier. Recognition of LTA reduction as one of several important indicators of safety performance—rather than *the* indicator—appears to be quite important.

Factory safety committees should be revised.

- More integration is needed between the plant safety committees and the departmental safety meetings.
- More emphasis should be placed on training rather than complaining and on communicating good safety practices to other workers.
- Safety committee members should be accorded a distinguishable status.
- Safety committees could provide a means of monitoring employee safety attitudes.

The factory safety committees were very effective in communicating management's concern for safety to members of the committee, but this safety attitude appeared not to have been achieved for noncommittee members.

One means of attaining safety consciousness on the part of a broader base of workers is to get more of them involved in the safety committees. However, efforts must also be made to extend the impact of the safety committee beyond its membership. A method that appears to have merit would be to involve the safety committee member as a formal liaison person between the committee and the departmental safety meetings. It was reported that training was at one time a formal part of factory safety committee meetings. This practice was halted because it appeared that only the committee members were benefiting from the training. It would seem imperative, therefore, that the linkage be made between the factory committee and the departmental meetings. Presently, factory committee meetings are devoted almost entirely to the complaints of the members concerning safety deficiencies. While such feedback is important, the training segment suggested here could serve to make the time spent at the meetings more constructive.

Collection of safety input figures should be more coordinated.

- Analysis and utilization of the "time" input should receive more emphasis.

While safety is said to be a major goal of the company, there is no safety budget for the plant. If safety is to be treated as a major goal, then statistics relating to safety spending should be collected in a unified manner for the purpose of adequate monitoring. Furthermore, since interpersonal contacts demand time away from production, usages of such time should be fully disclosed in the safety budget. Breakdowns of the time input could lead to the identification of those facets of the safety program implementation that are being under- or overutilized.

Measuring or monitoring of safety attitude change should be attempted.

- Attitude change might be more closely linked to off-the-job benefits of safety attitudes.
- Assumptions concerning the carryover of change to other goals should be reconsidered.

The measurement of employee safety consciousness as a sought-after goal was assumed to be reflected in the LTA indicator. The LTA did fall drastically, but no such improvement in safety attitudes was noted (except among members of the safety committee).

Changes in safety attitudes may be a long-term process, particularly for those who have equated safety with simply the absence of injury and have viewed production as their only real task. Provisions should be made to monitor and measure progress toward this goal. It was suggested earlier that the safety committee member might be a key figure in recording his perception of the safety concern of his fellow workers.

The worker can benefit off the job by working safely in the factory. By preventing injuries, he is able to maintain a steady flow of income and is psychologically and physically able to carry out familial obligations. Thus, the employee benefits by maintaining his safety consciousness off the job.

Improved safety attitudes may eventually foster such carryover benefits as are presently assumed by management. At present, though, management's efforts are largely perceived as being associated with OSHA and profit incentives. The carryover of improved employee morale can more logically be expected when management's concern for the employee as a person is better communicated to the employee. The carryovers of improved productivity and LTA reduction can be expected and better measured when safety criteria are more explicitly conveyed and when training procedures are made a more formal part of the implementation process.

Safety training of supervisors should be a priority concern.

Front-line supervisors are intimately connected with day-to-day operations. It is imperative that they be properly trained in correct safety procedures so that they can demonstrate how to put safety into action. The effective training of both supervisors and hourly employees is critical to accident reduction and might reduce the instances in which supervisors themselves ignore safety rules.

Changes are needed in the utilization of accident and safety reports.

- Management should utilize OSHA statistics in a more constructive manner.
- More control is needed over the conducting and reporting of departmental safety meetings.

OSHA statistics are presently accumulated because of the legal requirement to do so. It appears that management could begin to focus more attention on OSHA data, particularly OSHA calculations for disabling injuries.

As discussed earlier, the OSHA definition of a disabling injury—one that
renders the individual unable to perform regular duties—differs importantly from
the present ANSI standard, by which a disabling injury charge can be avoided
simply by having the victim perform another task. The ANSI standard can lead
to efforts to keep the injury from being charged rather than attempts to combat
future injuries.

It is not suggested that the company abandon the ANSI standard but
rather that management take a closer look at the OSHA statistics, which can
provide a good indication of where the company stands in regard to the law. A
favorable ANSI frequency may come to mean little if OSHA provisions become
more firmly institutionalized and more vigorously monitored.

Attention should also be directed toward the departmental safety meetings. The data analysis described in Section II indicated that these meetings have
been most effective in the prevention of accidents. However, many problems
had to be overcome in carrying out the analysis of the safety meeting forms.
Data requirements of the safety meeting report forms are different from the
requirements of the accident report forms, so an attempt to relate one activity
to another presents difficulties.

In light of the indicated benefits of the meetings, provisions should be
made to ensure that they are held more regularly and that the reporting system
is more adequately utilized.

---

*Recommended actions can be accomplished within the existing
cost structure of the safety program.*

This statement does not overlook the fact that changes in operations will
require initial costs of making the changes. The most notable start-up costs
would involve changes in accumulating safety budget data and costs of programing the computer for analysis of safety report forms. Similarly, there will be a
cost to make the information requirements of the report forms comparable.

For the most part, however, the recommended actions require very little
change in the operating costs of the safety program. In fact, even the changes in
the reporting system can be effected gradually. Furthermore, changes recommended for the safety committees can be accomplished without adding to the
time requirements of those meetings, as the recommendations call for alterations
in the use of time already allotted. Similarly, severity rates and OSHA statistics

are presently calculated; actions recommended call for changes in the ways the data are used. The greatest addition to operating costs involves the use of departmental safety meetings, but this is a cost to operationalize existing company policy that has been allowed to lapse in actual practice.

V: Limitations of the Audit

Attest to Reports

Reports relating to the safety program can be classified according to two types: those reporting various safety-related activities and those reporting specific accidents. In the first category are the minutes of the Factory Safety Committees and the Supervisory Report Forms from the departmental safety meetings. Accident reports include various OSHA forms, Accident Investigation Reports, and the Supervisory Report Form.

One function of the process audit has been to examine these reports and attest to their utilization. As has been indicated in earlier sections, it is possible to attest to the utilization of such reports only with certain qualifications. The utilization of departmental meeting forms was not consistent. Certain departments reported safety meetings consistently, and the reports were of good quality. Others either failed to hold meetings, or reported only a minimum of details. Because of the apparent lack of management control over the conducting and reporting of such meetings, it is difficult to draw any firm conclusions about the effectiveness of the reporting mechanism.

The Recommendations section also dealt at length with another aspect of the reporting system, the use of ANSI and OSHA standard statistics. We need mention only briefly here, therefore, that OSHA statistics have been accumulated solely for the purpose of providing information to the government. The accident reporting system is quite extensively utilized, but it focuses upon company-wide distribution of ANSI standard statistics to the exclusion of OSHA figures.

Evaluation of Approach

The process audit methodology utilized in this study exhibited recognizable strengths as well as weaknesses. Questions were asked about the safety program that had not been asked before. The approach sought to identify the major facets of the program process and to examine linkages among the elements of the program. The strengths of the report, however, require a proper perspective because of the uniqueness and newness of its application.

Many of the data were generated through interviews and observation. (Appendix 1 discusses the methods and procedures of data collection.) The audit team could not interview everyone in the company, nor could they be in all locations. To that extent, it is possible that very important information has been overlooked.

Dollar figures for expenditures relating to the safety program were very difficult to obtain. One apparent reason for this difficulty was an element of restraint exhibited by many of the respondents. Because of the newness of the approach, there was a perhaps natural and understandable tendency for those interviewed to refrain from volunteering information unless pressed for a response. In addition, dollar expenditure data for safety were not collected in a unified budget. Certain safety items were included in a repair and maintenance budget, others in a lost-time budget, and others in stockroom, medical, supplies, and other such budget classifications. As a result, some respondents stated that they could not themselves identify such expenditures.

Therefore, much of what is discussed in the way of input utilization is from the perspective of how inputs to the safety program might best be classified. Management should now be in a position to collect the input figures as suggested so that actual dollar amount comparisons can be made.

Data needs were discussed in the Recommendations section with regard to the development of more optimal accident prevention strategies. Many of the insights into the program resulting from analysis of safety records and accident reports required a very time-consuming process of coding report forms in order to make the information comparable. Equally time-consuming were efforts to track down expenditures data through various accounts, frequently without success. Consequently, there has been a long delay between the start of the audit and this report.

Such delays can adversely affect the timeliness of such a report for purposes of management control. However, future efforts would require much less time if such data as suggested are made readily available and if top management's support of the effort is effectively communicated. The fact that this process audit of the safety program has been carried out may have established in the minds of the respondents the need to scrutinize more closely the safety function. Future efforts to audit safety operations will, therefore, face less organizational resistance.

The weaknesses of the approach lie in the newness of the process audit methodology for all concerned. However, the audit has enabled those concerned to focus attention upon many important questions relating to safety. In addition, it has raised many questions that might not have been asked without this approach. Future efforts can begin to focus on the unanswered questions that the present study has brought to light.

Appendix 6.E. Process Audit Rationale

Appendix 1 Methods of Data Collection
EXHIBIT A: Interview Schedule (Social Audit Research Group—Company Safety Program)
EXHIBIT B: Short Form Interview Schedule

Appendix 2 Methods of Analysis of Safety Report Forms

Epilogue and Update

The social audit of this safety program was undertaken about two and a half years ago at a company that was in the process of developing and implementing a new loss prevention program. Consequently, the results reported here are based on a corporate effort that was undergoing and has undergone significant change. We have been told by company officials that some of the findings and recommendations in our report have resulted in revised policies and procedures. Moreover, the company itself has instituted various changes that make the current program even better than the well-planned one on which the report is based.

Several of the revisions are worth mentioning. Currently, clear safety goals are established for each factory manager, and the manager's success in achieving the goals is examined in his or her performance review. This represents an important attempt to institutionalize the importance of effective performance in the area of safety. To aid the manager in these safety concerns, the company is developing the computer capability to analyze various safety figures, observe trends, and uncover specific problem areas. The computer analyses will be made available to all relevant managers. In addition, the company has organized its accounts so that there is currently a budgeted Safety Department at each factory. This move has provided for the linking of performance with cost figures and enables responsible managers to assess more readily the effectiveness of funds spent on various types of safety activities.

The audit report emphasized the importance of the safety meetings in making members more alert to the need for safety. The company has taken steps to ensure that these are held and that the reports of the meetings are submitted on a uniform basis to the Safety Department head for his subsequent analysis. This is one more example of the company's efforts to establish a safety program that is as well managed as any other function of the company.

In conclusion, though, it needs to be stressed that the proceding report was intended to illustrate what a social audit does and is designed to accomplish. The reader should obtain from this example insight into the nature of a social process audit and how it can be useful to other companies and other programs.

7

SOCIAL AUDITING:
A PRACTICAL
MANAGEMENT TOOL

Our purpose in the foregoing chapters has been twofold. First, we have sought to develop and explain in comprehensive form a methodology, the necessary implementation procedures, and a suitable reporting format for use in conducting a social process audit. These steps have not previously been set forth in such detail, nor, prior to our work, had they been so carefully tailored to meet the organizational needs of professional managers. The need for such managerially oriented social audit techniques has been recognized by leading scholars in the field of social auditing, especially Professors Raymond Bauer and Dan Fenn, Jr. of Harvard University.* When we began our work in 1972, there were few theoretical guidelines and no practical experience regarding the social process audit upon which to draw. Necessity, indeed, became the mother of our inventions of a methodology, implementation techniques, and a report format. They are offered here for those managers who believe it important and worthwhile to determine in a systematic and analytic fashion just how their companies affect their communities. Academic scholars, also, will wish to examine the usefulness, as well as the limitations, of these social audit tools.

Our second purpose, closely related to the first, has been to report the experience of the University of Pittsburgh's Social Audit Research Group in actually conducting two social process audits within a large corporation, so as to illustrate directly the practical usefulness of this new tool of corporate social

---

*See Raymond A. Bauer and Dan H. Fenn, Jr., *The Corporate Social Audit* (New York: Russell Sage Foundation, 1972); and, by the same authors, "What *Is* a Corporate Social Audit?" *Harvard Business Review*, January-February 1973.

policy. As we have emphasized over and over, social auditing can and ought to be used as a practical decision-making aid by organizational managers. Only when it becomes obvious that social auditing can be a useful guide to organizational decision making will this new technique be accepted into the regular routines of major companies. We have sought to demonstrate that not only is it possible to conduct social audits within a major business corporation but also that the results of those audits are of practical benefit to management.

For those persons who hold a skeptical or cynical view of the social attitudes and practices of large corporations, it might be instructive to note the warm and open invitation extended to the members of the Social Audit Research Group to enter the company and to choose among several areas ripe for social auditing. As the audits proceeded over a period of several months, the audit teams enjoyed the full cooperation of management in implementing the studies, with no serious hitches in obtaining necessary data when requested. Upon completion of the two audits, management received them gratefully as a welcome supplement to previous knowledge. And as noted in the preceding chapter, some important changes have subsequently been made in both the industrial safety program and the philanthropic contributions program. These changes parallel various recommendations contained in the two audits. We believe that both programs are now administered more effectively than in pre-audit times, that more and better communication prevails, that management perception and thinking about the programs' goals are clearer, and that the social groups affected by both programs are, as a consequence of these changes, better served by the company. We hasten to say that these impressions of social betterment cannot be verified by completely scientific means, nor do we wish to imply that they might have occurred only as a result of our social auditing activities. This company is a progressive one, peopled by many managers not only alert to traditional business values but fully aware of corporate social impacts and social needs.

Our study and this book can be most clearly understood if viewed as one stage in the emergence both of social auditing as a management tool and of the larger area of corporate social policy and practice. Our research group chose to get into the field and actually conduct some research rather than to talk about the unending difficulties and obstacles that one might encounter in doing so. We also believed that more value would come from an experiment, positively and openly conducted, than from abstract speculation, negatively and pessimistically projected.

The overall results are recorded in the text. We encountered most of the technical and conceptual difficulties that have been widely discussed and wisely noted by numerous scholars. A clear consensus regarding the appropriate social criteria to be brought to bear in most social areas is lacking. It is not easy, for example, to decide "how safe" a factory should be, or "how clean" the air and water should be made, or "how equal" an employment policy should be. We also found, as others have before us, that some of the most critical elements that enter into the assessment of a company's social activities cannot be measured by quantitative yardsticks and that this shortcoming limits the types of analyses that can be carried out. What quantitative weight, for example, should one give to the personalized goals and satisfactions of a socially conscientious staff administering a philanthropic contributions program? To say that such personal elements, because they cannot be quantified, are to be treated as irrelevant in the overall assessment of the program is to omit one of the vital energizing components of the entire activity. These and similar obstacles do definitely exist and will complicate the life of the social auditor.

However, two mitigating developments provide a basis for believing that social auditing will finally emerge as a full-fledged tool of management decision making. The very existence of this present study, with its audit methodology, the implementation techniques, and the report format, signal that some useful progress is possible and has been accomplished. No doubt, as we ourselves have pointed out, imperfections exist, improvements can and should be made, and the progress has at best been modest in overall proportion to the need. But still in this limited manner, the techniques of social process auditing have been carried to a new stage of development, well beyond where they were only a short three or four years ago. No longer can it be said that social auditing from a managerial viewpoint is merely a theoretical possibility. Anyone—professional manager or academic scholar—who is interested in social auditing now has a tangible example of how the social process audit looks in actual practice. We believe that such a concrete illustration, built as it is on the solid experiences of an actual company anxious to know more about its social impacts, augurs well for sharpening and refining the tools of social auditing in the future.

A second factor holding some promise that social auditing may become an accepted management practice is that social auditing—whether one considers the social process type or one of the several others being tried out—is only one of several new approaches being made to the broad area of corporate social policy and practice. Additionally, one finds rich and burgeoning developments in such areas as technology assessment, social indicators, cost-benefit analysis, sociopolitical forecasting, and other related endeavors. In broad outline, each one of these interesting movements represents an attempt to systematize our understanding of social values and to find ways to translate that better understanding into tangible social policy and practice. It is quite likely that as advances are made in one of these fields, progress will occur in others as a result. We noted in an earlier chapter that the rapidly expanding field of social indicators may well in time begin to provide enough social information to enable communities to evolve a somewhat systematic set of social criteria that can be used to judge the performance of individual organizations and governmental units. In such circumstances, social audits of individual companies could provide the detailed look at specific, identifiable social impacts that might register either positively or negatively on one or more of these social indicators.

All of these social policy tools, including social auditing, are likely to become increasingly important aids to management decision making as more and more large-scale organizations in both the private and public sectors attempt to ameliorate their impacts upon the communities in which they operate. Some companies appear now to be taking the initial steps to acquaint themselves with the opportunities, as well as the pitfalls, of these new corporate social policy tools.

Finally, the experience of our Social Audit Research Group carries one lesson of overriding importance. Tangible steps can be taken to advance a new field or an untried tool in spite of technical and conceptual difficulties that may exist and that may seem inherently defeating. Waiting for perfection in the field of social auditing is a bit like "waiting for Godot"—who, in the play by that title, never comes. Professional managers need and deserve pioneering aid and the fruits of bold experiments if they are to confront today's and tomorrow's social problems and pressures with any degree of success and humaneness. Professional schools of management can and should work to extend such aid and to engage in such experimentation. Our work is one example among many of how a fruitful relationship can exist between management scholars and management practitioners that simultaneously advances a scholarly field of inquiry and the practice of management.

SOCIAL AUDIT MODELS

In Chapter 2 we briefly described several different approaches to social auditing. Although the primary emphasis of our book is upon the social process audit, we present in this appendix three contrasting types of social audits so that the interested reader, whether academic scholar or management practitioner, may compare them in greater detail.

The three social audit models have been developed by Clark C. Abt of Abt Associates, Inc., David F. Linowes of Laventhal and Horwarth, and James L. Hetland, Jr. and James M. Williams of the First National Bank of Minneapolis. All three types of audits are, or have been at some time, in use in a business corporation. Each one represents an initial effort to put into practice the theory of social auditing and to grapple with the problems of social measurement in a creative and productive way.

In addition to these three models, there are other social auditing initiatives that have been undertaken and that are not included here for lack of space. Some of these audits—such as those employed by the Equal Employment Opportunity Commission—are designed for special purposes and have had extensive use in many types of organizations.

We remain convinced, though, that the social process audit is and will continue to be the most useful managerial approach to social auditing.

THE ABT MODEL

Social audits evaluate an organization's social impacts on its constituencies—the staff, the clients, the owners, the neighboring community, and the general public. These impacts are expressed in money units of cumulative and yearly benefits and costs.

The social concerns addressed by the 1974 Social Audit include productivity, contribution to knowledge, employment security, fairness of employment opportunities, health, education and self-development, physical security, transportation, recreation, and environment.

From Annual Report and Social Audit 1974, Abt Associates Inc., pp. 17-22. Courtesy of Abt Associates, Inc., Cambridge, Massachusetts.

Abt Associates Inc. Social and Financial Balance Sheet

Assets (Note 1)	1974	1973
Staff		
Staff Available Within One Year (Note 2)	$ 7,555,000	6,384,000
Staff Available After One Year (Note 3)	14,895,000	15,261,000
Training Investment (Note 4)	2,986,000	2,051,000
	25,436,000	23,696,000
Less Accumulated Training		
Obsolescence (Note 4)	1,422,000	503,000
Total	$24,014,000	23,193,000
Organization		
Creation and Development of Organization		
Research (Note 5)	$ 554,000	437,000
Child Care Development	25,000	7,000
Social Audit Development	46,000	32,000
Total	$ 625,000	476,000
General Public and Community		
Public Services Paid For Through Taxes		
(Net of Consumption) (Note 6)	$ 839,000	365,000
Total	$ 839,000	365,000
Stockholders		
Cash	$ 27,000	91,000
Accounts Receivable Less Allowance for		
Doubtful Accounts	1,567,000	2,083,000
Unbilled Contract Cost and Fees	1,886,000	1,789,000
Other Current Financial Assets	169,000	42,000
Other Long-Term Financial Assets	6,000	39,000
Total	$ 3,655,000	4,044,000
Physical Assets:		
Recreation Center	$ 106,000	0
Land and Improvements	467,000	310,000
Buildings and Improvements	3,649,000	2,157,000
Equipment, Furniture, and Fixtures	430,000	242,000
Total Fixed Assets	4,652,000	2,709,000
Less Accumulated Depreciation	336,000	204,000
Total	$ 4,316,000	2,505,000
Total	$33,449,000	30,583,000

Liabilities (Note 7)	1974	1973	Equity	1974	1973
	Staff				
Staff Wages Payable (Note 8)	**$24,014,000**	23,193,000	See statement below for staff financial equity that is not a social asset or social liability.		
	$24,014,000	23,193,000		0	0
	Organization				
Organizational Financing Requirement (Note 9)	**$ 1,056,000**	563,000			
	$ 1,056,000	563,000		(431,000)	(87,000)
	General Public and Community				
Environmental Resources Used Through Pollution:					
Paper	**$ 18,000**	11,000			
Electricity	**113,000**	76,000			
Commuting	**58,000**	37,000			
	$ 189,000	124,000		650,000	241,000
	Stockholders				
Notes Payable (Current)	**$ 406,000**	514,000	Staff Stockholders Equity:		
Accounts Payable & Accrued Expenses	**788,000**	1,081,000	Common Stock	**95,000**	95,000
Accrued Expenses	**1,059,000**	875,000	Additional Paid-In Capital	**480,000**	480,000
Federal Income Taxes	**24,000**	109,000	Retained Earnings	**444,000**	249,000
Deferred Federal Income Taxes	**98,000**	52,000	Total	**$1,019,000**	824,000
Notes Payable (Long-Term)	**1,300,000**	1,092,000	Non-Staff Stockholders Equity:		
Leasehold Interest in Property	**130,000**	128,000	Common Stock	**200,000**	200,000
			Additional Paid-In Capital	**1,011,000**	1,011,000
			Retained Earnings	**936,000**	618,000
			Total	**$2,147,000**	1,829,000
	$ 4,805,000	3,851,000			
	$30,064,000	27,731,000		**$3,385,000**	2,807,000

151

Abt Associates Inc. Social and Financial Income Statement

Benefits	1974	1973
Company/Stockholders		
Contract Revenue and Other Income (Note 10)	$16,423,000	15,224,000
Federal Services Consumed (Note 11)	262,000	195,000
State Services Consumed	104,000	80,000
Local Services Consumed	40,000	32,000
Environmental Resources Used Through Pollution (Note 12)		
Electricity	37,000	35,000
Commuting	21,000	17,000
Paper	7,000	6,000
Total	$16,894,000	15,589,000
Staff		
Salaries Paid for Time Worked (Note 13)	$ 6,231,000	5,399,000
Career Advancement (Note 20)	700,000	602,000
Vacation and Holidays	719,000	571,000
Health and Life Insurance	461,000	361,000
Sick Leave	185,000	127,000
Retirement Income Plan	50,000	0
Parking	95,000	124,000
Tuition Reimbursement	15,000	2,000
Food Service (Note 21)	67,000	51,000
Quality of Work Space (Note 22)	134,000	16,000
Child Care	18,000	11,000
Credit Union	11,000	8,000
Recreation Center	27,000	0
Total	$ 8,713,000	7,272,000
Clients		
Value of Contract Research (Note 28)	$16,423,000	15,224,000
Professional Staff Overtime Worked But Not Paid (Note 29)	1,184,000	1,056,000
Federal Taxes Paid by Company	474,000	349,000
State and Federal Tax Worth of Net Jobs Created (Note 30)	96,000	327,000
State Taxes Paid By Company	130,000	100,000
Contribution to Knowledge (Note 31)	60,000	54,000
Total	18,367,000	17,110,000
Community		
Local Taxes Paid by Company	$ 78,000	63,000
Local Tax Worth of Net Jobs Created	16,000	52,000
Environmental Improvements	36,000	18,000
Reduced Parking Area (Note 35)	29,000	0
Total	$ 159,000	133,000
Total	$44,133,000	40,104,000

Costs	1974	1973	Net Benefits	1974	1973
Salaries Paid (Exclusive of Training (Note 13)					
Investment and Fringe Benefits) (Note 14)	$ 5,296,000	4,319,000			
Training Investment in Staff	935,000	1,080,000			
Direct Contract Cost	5,529,000	5,596,000			
Overhead/General Administrative Expenditures					
Not Itemized	1,860,000	1,649,000			
Vacation and Holidays	719,000	571,000			
Improvements, Space and Environment (Note 15)	137,000	384,000			
Federal Taxes Paid (Note 16)	474,000	349,000			
State Taxes Paid (Note 16)	130,000	100,000			
Local Taxes Paid (Note 16)	78,000	63,000			
Health and Life Insurance	256,000	201,000			
Sick Leave	185,000	127,000			
Food Service	67,000	51,000			
Child Care	18,000	11,000			
Tuition Reimbursement	15,000	2,000			
Miscellaneous and Public Offering of Stock	0	154,000			
Interest Payments (Note 17)	197,000	171,000			
Income Foregone on Paid in Capital (Note 18)	265,000	276,000			
	$16,161,000	15,104,000		733,000	485,000
Opportunity Cost of Total Time Worked (Note 23)	$ 7,540,000	6,455,000			
Absence of Retirement Income Plan (Note 24)	1,000	58,000			
Layoffs and Involuntary Terminations (Note 25)	77,000	31,000			
Inequality of Opportunity (Note 26)	1,000	11,000			
Uncompensated Losses Through Theft	1,000	1,000			
Reduced Parking Area (Note 27)	29,000	0			
	$ 7,649,000	6,556,000		1,064,000	716,000
Cost of Contract Work to Client (Note 32)	$16,423,000	15,224,000			
Federal Services Consumed (Note 33)	262,000	195,000			
State Services Consumed (Note 33)	104,000	80,000			
Environmental Resources Used Through Pollution:					
(Note 34)					
Electricity	37,000	35,000			
Commuting	21,000	17,000			
Paper	7,000	6,000			
	$16,854,000	15,557,000		1,513,000	1,553,000
Local Services Consumed	$ 40,000	32,000			
	40,000	32,000		119,000	101,000
	$40,704,000	37,249,000		$3,429,000	2,855,000

Why do a social audit? We do social audits to obtain guidance in making management decisions affecting our social performance. We present the results of our social audit to show the social impacts of our management decisions.

What is new about social audits is the measurement of the *net* social impacts of an organization in quantitative terms, comparable from year to year, item to item, company to company. This quantification aids decisions concerning human resources and capital investments, operating practices, and management policies. For example, specific decisions made in response to our social audits include initiation of a retirement plan, dental insurance, visiting social scientists, expanded educational opportunities, and salary adjustments. Efficient choices among socially relevant alternatives are aided by the relative benefit-cost estimates provided by social audits.

Social audits complement the financial information provided by conventional accounting with social performance information. The integration of social and financial reports allows for a more direct comparison of social and financial benefits and costs. Abt Associates Inc.'s 1974 Social Audit is in a new format intended to clarify benefit-cost comparison, but the line items and methods of computation are substantially the same as those used in 1973.

The procedures used in the 1974 Social Audit were: (1) surveys of the stockholders, staff, clients, and the host community to identify the major social concerns for determining the relevant line items and perceived values; (2) quantification of items in terms of their market or perceived dollar values; (3) computation of net social incomes by subtracting the sum of the social costs from the sum of the social benefits for each constituency. Net social incomes are distributed as they are created; they do not flow into the social balance sheet since such social earnings are not retained; and, (4) computation of a social equity on the social balance sheet by subtracting the sum of social liabilities from the social assets.

The 1974 Social Audit was conducted by Dr. Clark C. Abt, Dr. Donald Muse, and Mr. Neal Perry.

For more details on the calculations see the notes on the 1973 Social Audit in Abt Associates 1973 Annual Report, or write the company for detailed notes on how the Social Audit values were determined.

1. <u>Social assets</u> are resources which promise to provide future social or economic benefits, and are a social asset to the company valued at their present worth.

2. <u>Staff available within one year</u> are staff immediately available to provide research and evaluation services, estimated to be $7,555,000 for 1974 based on a discount rate of .9715 and a mean staff tenure of 2.95 years. For 1973, staff assets were valued at $6,384,000 based on a discount rate of .9604 and a mean staff tenure of 3.8 years.

3. <u>Staff available after one year</u> is estimated to be $14,895,000 for 1974 based on a discount rate of 1.915 and a mean staff tenure of 2.95 years. For 1973, staff assets after one year were based on a discount rate of 2.296 and a mean staff tenure of 3.8 years.

4. <u>Training investment</u> in staff is a social asset that promises to provide present and future benefits. The 1974 staff survey indicated that company staff spent an average 15 percent of their time in training, decreasing from a high of 25 percent five years ago to 10 percent this year. <u>Accumulated training obsolescence</u> is a reduction in total training based on a straightline depreciation of training investment over the mean staff tenure.

5. <u>Creation and development of organization</u> is an organizational asset equated to the replacement cost of paid-in capital, computed by weighing the capital stock account from 1965 to the present by the deflator for Gross Private Fixed investment.

6. <u>Public services paid by taxes but not consumed</u> by the company are social assets to the general public and the community. When the company consumes fewer public services than paid by taxes, a net social asset is produced.

7. <u>Social liabilities</u> are sources of future economic or social cost and are valued at their present economic worth.

8. <u>Staff wages payable</u> are a liability contingent upon future utilization of staff on contract or administrative tasks. This amount does not constitute a liability in the legal sense but it does show expected future liability to pay staff as they provide future services.

9. <u>Organizational financing requirements cost</u> is equated to the difference between mean borrowing during the year and year-end borrowing which was $1,056,000 for 1974, compared to $563,000 for 1973.

10. <u>Contract revenue and other income</u> is a social benefit to the company and the stockholders because it results in a direct economic benefit and payment to the company.

11. <u>Federal services consumed</u> by the company are a social benefit to the company and the stockholders because the federal services contributed to the operations.

12. Environmental resources creating pollution are a social benefit to the company and the stockholders because the company earns economic benefits by production processes creating socially undesirable environmental effects without paying for them.

13. Salaries paid exclusive of training investment and fringe benefits are a social cost to the company and stockholders because payment for staff services reduces available company funds, and once spent for staff services these funds cannot be used again for other services.

14. Training investment in staff is a social cost to the company and stockholders which results in a loss of staff time during training and a loss of funds paid to staff during training time when the staff was nonproductive.

15. Improvements, space, and environment expenditures are a social and economic cost to the company and stockholders because money spent on building maintenance is not available for other uses by the company.

16. Federal, state, and local taxes paid by the company are a social and economic cost to the company and stockholders because tax payments reduce the amount of money available for other uses.

17. Interest payments are a social and economic cost to the company and stockholders because the amount spent to borrow money cannot be expensed to contract work and therefore is a loss and cannot be used for other purposes.

18. Income foregone on paid-in capital is a social and economic cost to the stockholders because of having paid-in capital tied up in the company.

19. Salaries paid to staff for time worked are a social benefit to the staff members because it results in a direct economic benefit in payment for their contribution to company operations.

20. Career advancement is a social benefit to the staff because of the added earning power from salary increases for merit or promotion.

21. Food service subsidy by the company is a social benefit to the staff because it increases the quality of food served to the staff on the premises above that commercially available for the same prices.

22. Quality of work space is a social benefit to the staff created by the above average office space provided employees.

23. Opportunity cost of total time worked is a social cost to staff because it represents time given up while working for the company.

24. Absence of retirement plan is a social cost to the staff for 1973. In 1974 a retirement plan was implemented. Only four eligible staff who terminated early in the year experienced any social cost as a result of plan absence when they left.

25. Layoffs and involuntary terminations is a social cost to the staff. A survey was take of the 72 terminees that showed that 45 percent of terminees were still unemployed after 60 days. Social cost is estimated to be one month's salary for the 40 terminees who found employment within 60 days and two

months' salary for the 32 terminees who found employment after 60 days.

26. Inequality of opportunity is a social cost to the staff and is defined in terms of the costs to individuals of the income loss equal to the difference between what the minority or female individual earns and what a nonminority or male individual doing the same job with the same qualifications earns.

27. Reduced parking area is a social cost to the staff in the Cambridge office that drive automobiles. The company reduced the number of parking spaces by 80 in order to comply with Environmental Protection Agency requirements that all companies in the area reduce their parking areas.

28. Value of contract research as a social benefit is assumed to be whatever is paid for the service, since it was purchased on the open market.

29. Staff overtime worked but not paid is a social benefit to society and the client and constitutes an "invisible subsidy" by the company professional staff that results in a higher quality of services. The 1974 staff survey showed a decrease of overtime to 19% of regular working hours from 20% in 1973 and 33% in 1972.

30. State and federal tax worth of net jobs created are a social benefit to the general public because each new job will create additional tax revenue for the state and federal government. Expansion of the company has created 67 new jobs in Cambridge.

31. Contribution to knowledge is a social benefit to the general public because publications by the company staff constitute additions to the stock of knowledge.

32. Cost of contract research is a social cost to the client and the general public because payment for research comes from state and federal governments which reduces the amount of money available for other uses.

33. Federal and state services consumed are a social cost to the general public and society from the company's use of public services.

34. Environmental resources used through pollution are a social cost to the general public and society caused by socially undesirable effects of production that are not paid for by the company.

35. Reduced parking areas is a social benefit to the local community resulting in less pollution and traffic on the highway.

AN APPROACH TO SOCIO-ECONOMIC ACCOUNTING

David F. Linowes

...What we might do at once, then, is to borrow from economics and apply the "system" of economic and fiscal measurement to social areas. It is this that I call Socio-Economic Measurement.

Dollars involving social costs incurred by business are equally determinable. However, the fact that a prepared statement of these costs may not be complete is not sufficient reason for us to delay further the preparation and use of such exhibits. Traditional financial statements have never themselves been able to reflect significant facets of business affairs fully—e.g., contingent assets such as the value of trained manpower, extent of provision for executive succession, potential profitability of new inventions and product development, or contingent liabilities which include potential adverse legal actions for faulty products.

Measuring Social "Detriments" and "Improvements"

There should be no reason to forbid us from developing a Socio-Economic Operating Statement (SEOS). It would be prepared periodically along with a business organization's profit and loss statement and balance sheet. The SEOS I visualize is a tabulation of those expenditures made voluntarily by a business aimed at the "improvement" of the welfare of the employees and public, safety of the product, and/or conditions of the environment. Such expenditures required by law or union contract would not be includable, inasmuch as these are mandatory and necessary costs of doing business.

An item is determined to be a "detriment" or negative charge for SEOS purposes when a responsible authority brings the need for social action to the attention of management, but management does not voluntarily take steps to satisfy such a need, even though it is of such a nature that a reasonably prudent and socially aware business management would have responded favorably. The fact that this determination is a subjective one should not discourage its implementation. In traditional business accounting, research and development items, work in process inventories, allowances for bad debts, depreciation charges, price-earnings ratios are also largely subjective determinations.

From *The Conference Board Record*, volume IX, number 11, November 1972, pp. 58-61.

Several guidelines to help identify and classify socio-economic items can be offered:

- If a socially beneficial action is required by law, but is ignored, the cost of such item is a "detriment" for the year. The same treatment is given an item if postponed, even with government approval. Similarly, if a socially beneficial action is required by law and is applied earlier than the law requires, it is an improvement. (In an inflationary period this might mean a saving of money for the company and could be categorized as a contingent asset.)
- A pro-rata portion of salaries and related expenses of personnel who spent time in socially beneficial actions or with social organizations is included as an "improvement."
- Cash and product contributions to social institutions are included as "improvements."
- Cost of setting up facilities for the general good of employees or the public—without union or government requirement—is an includable "improvement."
- Neglecting to install safety devices which are available at a reasonable cost is a "detriment."
- The cost of voluntarily building a playground or nursery school for employees and/or neighbors is a plus on the exhibit. Operating costs of the facility in each succeeding year are also includable.
- Costs of relandscaping strip mining sites, or other environmental eyesores, if not otherwise required by law, are listed as improvements on the SEOS exhibit.
- Extra costs in designing and building unusually attractive business facilities for beauty, health and safety are includable "improvements."

The results of a Socio-Economic Operating Statement produce an amount of "Total Socio-Economic Contribution or Deficit for the Year." It can be effectively used by comparing such statements for various companies in the same industry. Also, analyzing SEO Statements for a particular company over several years helps establish the general directions of the social involvement of a company's management.

The Social Audit as an Operating Statement

The various positive and negative social actions and inactions mentioned are classified on the SEOS exhibit into three groups: relations with people, relations with environment, and relations with product. The Socio-Economic Operating Statement that I recommend be instituted is illustrated by the Table below.

XXXX CORPORATION

Socio-Economic Operating Statement for the Year Ending December 31, 1971

I Relations with People:

A. Improvements:

1. Training program for handicapped workers — $10,000
2. Contribution to educational institution — 4,000
3. Extra turnover costs because of minority hiring program — 5,000
4. Cost of nursery school for children of employees, voluntarily set up — 11,000

Total Improvements — $30,000

B. Less: Detriments

1. Postponed installing new safety devices on cutting machines (cost of the devices) — $14,000

C. Net Improvements in People Actions for the Year — $16,000

II Relations with Environment:

A. Improvements:

1. Cost of reclaiming and landscaping old dump on company property — $70,000
2. Cost of installing pollution control devices on Plant A smokestacks — 4,000
3. Cost of detoxifying waste from finishing process this year — 9,000

Total Improvements — $83,000

B. Less: Detriments

1. Cost that would have been incurred to relandscape strip mining site used this year — $80,000
2. Estimated costs to have installed purification process to neutralize poisonous liquid being dumped into stream — $100,000 — $180,000

C. Net Deficit in Environment Actions for the Year — ($ 97,000)

III Relations with Product:

A. Improvements

1. Salary of V.P. while serving on government Product Safety Commission — 25,000
2. Cost of substituting lead-free paint for previously used poisonous lead paint — 9,000 — $ 34,000

B. Less: Detriments

1. Safety device recommended by Safety Council but not added to product — 22,000

C. Net Improvements in Product Actions for the Year — $ 12,000

Total Socio-Economic Deficit for the Year — ($69,000)

Net Cumulative Socio-Economic Improvements as of January 1, 1971 — 249,000

GRAND TOTAL NET SOCIO-ECONOMIC ACTIONS TO DECEMBER 31, 1971 — $180,000

Preparing the Socio-Economic Operating Statement

The SEOS exhibits themselves would be prepared by a small inter-disciplinary team headed by an accountant. Other members of the team could include a seasoned business executive, sociologist, public health administrator, economist, or members of other disciplines whose specific expertise might apply to a particular industry or circumstance. Although SEO Statements would be prepared internally by an interdisciplinary group, they should be audited by an outside independent interdisciplinary team headed by a CPA.

Though determination of items to be included in the SEOS is to be based upon subjective judgments, a standard dollar value applied to these improvements or "detriments" would be a combination of what businessmen traditionally classify as capital expenditures and expense expenditures. For example, the full cost of a permanent installation of a pollution control device is included in the SEO Statement in the year the cost is voluntarily incurred, as is the annual operating cost of a minority group training program. For convenience of reference, the totals could be expressed in Socio-Economic Management Dollars (SEM$) so as to identify all expenditures made voluntarily of a socially beneficial nature.

Specific cost items which would be entered on a SEOS as "improvements" or positive actions would include: 1. cost of training program for handicapped workers; 2. contribution to educational institutions; 3. extra turnover costs because of minority hiring policy. (the adverse of this item, the cost of not setting up adequate orientation programs, would be included as detrimental nonactions); (4) cost of nursery school for children of employees, voluntarily set up; (5) cost of reclaiming and landscaping old dump on company property; (6) cost of installing pollution control devices on smokestacks ahead of legal requirements; (7) cost of detoxifying waste from finishing process this year, ahead of legal requirement; (8) salary of vice president while serving on government Product Safety Commission; and, (9) cost of substituting lead-free paint for previously used poisonous lead paint.

Contrariwise, these specific costs would be entered on the SEOS as negative or detrimental nonactions: 1. postponed installing new safety devices on cutting machines (cost of the devices); 2. cost that would have been incurred to relandscape strip mining site used this year; 3. estimated cost to have installed a purification process to neutralize polluting liquid being dumped into stream; and, 4. cost of safety device recommended by Safety Council but not added to product.

I would emphasize that some of these examples may no longer be includable on a current Socio-Economic Operating Statement, but they serve to illustrate.

THE FIRST MINNEAPOLIS BANK MODEL

1974 Social-Environmental Audit

Public confidence in business, governmental and public institutions remains dangerously low. The public knows that business decisions have a substantial effect on society, but does not know what those decisions are and whether the impact is positive or negative. Since all businesses exist and prosper at the sufferance of the public, there must be a better mutual understanding of the relationship between business decisions and society's expectations.

One step toward a better understanding is to report accurately the total business function to all constituencies served by business. Through such a report business leaders can see factually what impacts exist, what programs work and do not work and what allocation should be made of business resources to address specific community needs. Critics will know precisely what has been achieved, what has not been achieved and the reasons. Legislative and governmental regulators can make decisions on the basis of fact, rather than emotion. The key to such a reporting system is a measurement method accurately reflecting total corporate activity.

In recognition of this need First National Bank of Minneapolis in 1972 and 1973 created a Social-Environmental Audit designed to measure business impact in specific categories of community concern.

The Social-Environmental Audit serves two important functions: (1) it identifies, measures and reports to the corporation's major constituencies the social costs and the social benefits of doing business; (2) it furnishes corporate policy makers with social impact information which, in turn, can be used in corporate decision making and long-term planning.

First Minneapolis published its first Social-Environmental Audit as an integral part of the bank annual report in an attempt to state the impact of total banking activity as it affected the public, customers, shareholders and bank employees. That accounting was preceded by a 1972 First Minneapolis audit of community needs and priorities. The community audit also provided the bank with substantial experience and experimentation in various measurement methods. It also showed a clear need for public statistics which measure results and achievements rather than merely inputs and programs. The 1974 Social-Environmental Audit follows the format of the 1973 report. The audit again

Reproduced by permission. First National Bank of Minneapolis, Minneapolis, Minnesota; James L. Hetland, Jr., Vice President, and James M. Williams, Urban Development Representative, Urban Development Department.

identifies principal areas affecting the quality of life in the Minneapolis-St. Paul metropolitan region. It then measures, through use of result-oriented indicators, the quality and quantity of the bank's activity in each area. Totaling two or more of the indicators in a single account tends to reflect a present status of that particular account.

Management Through Commitment (MTC) objectives reflect the yearly corporate plan and implementation strategy for each indicator. The plan is set by evaluation of community need and evaluation of bank resources that properly can be allocated to each need. Within the audit the Social Performance index reflects the degree to which objectives have been accomplished.

For 1975 corporate planning and objectives have been correlated with the audit for the purpose of producing a more complete Performance index.

Comparison with prior year performance indicators reflects activities over a longer time period or represents changes in community or bank priorities.

Finding key result-oriented indicators for some accounts again proved troublesome. The income account was uniquely difficult because of the extraordinary inflation in 1974. Public concerns changed markedly from 1973 because of economic conditions which affected indicators for the Consumer Protection-Service account.

A major objective for 1975 is to relate performance in each of the accounts in such a way that a net social gain or loss can be reported, coupled with an evaluation of the relative success or failure between one or more components.

1974 Internal Social-Environmental Audit

FIRST NATIONAL BANK OF MINNEAPOLIS

		1974 Performance Level	Net Percentage Performance Differential '73-74 (2)	1974 Objectives (3)	1974 Social Performance Index (4)	1975 Objectives (5)
Housing 1 (1)	1. Number of residential mortgage loans originated in 1974 to families living in	a.) 360	35%	+	↑	a.) 360
	a.) Minneapolis b.) Suburbs & St. Paul	b.) 967	30	+	↓	b.) 967
	2. Dollar amount of residential mortgage loans originated in 1974 to families in	a.) $ 8.861.000	25	+	↑	a.) $ 8.861,000
	a.) Minneapolis b.) Suburbs & St. Paul	b.) $29.324,000	20	+	↑	b.) $29,324,000
	3. Number of outstanding home improvement loans made to families living in	a.) 357	15			a.) 655
	a.) Minneapolis b.) Suburbs & St. Paul	b.) 744	10			b.) 676
	4. Ratio originated residential mortgage loans to bank's total resources	1:50	5			1:50
	5. Foundation contribution	$10.000	0	$10,920	.92	$10,000
Education 2	1. Number of classes taken by employees paid by bank	363	5%	+	↓	
	a.) internal	164	4	+	↑	
	b.) external	199		+	↓	
	2. Number of employees in bank college gift matching program	48	3	+	↑	55
	3. Employee community involvement man-hours per month	1.129	2	+	↑	1,241
	4. Foundation contribution to educational institutions	$51.750	1 / 0	$50.006	1.03	$55,000
Public Safety 3	1. Accidents on bank premises involving employees — 1974 (Does not include sports)	26	80% / 60 / 40			26
	2. Accidents involving non-employees	14	20 / 0			14
Income 4	1. Clerical employees — monthly income related to area-wide averages	1:1.01				1:1
	2. Clerical employees — composite productivity relation to base 1973	1:1.06				1:1.10
Job Opportunities 5	1. Percent officers, managers and professionals (EEO defined)	a.) 19.8	80%	+	↑	a.) 23.8
	a.) women b.) racial minority	b.) 3.5	60	+	↑	b.) 4.2
	2. Percent of job categories posted	77	20 / 0	75	1.03	77
Health 6	1. Estimated commitment to treatment of alcoholism a.) money b.) man-hours	a.) $5.460 b.) 222	50%	+ 50% +100%	.61 1.39	
	2. Number of days missed due to health problems per capita	a.) 3.43	40	a.) 5.0	a.) 1.7	a.) 3.43
	a.) women b.) men	b.) 1.65	30	b.) 2.3	b.) 4.3	b.) 1.65
	3. Prepaid health services (HMO) as employee health option		20			
	a.) services offered	a.) 0				a.) 0
	b.) dollar	b.) $1,000	10	+	↓	b.) $1,500
	c.) man-hours	c.) 141	0	+	↑	c.) 150
Transportation 7	1. Percent employees taking bus to work	61	50% / 40	50	1.22	65
	2. Percent employees who come to work in car pools	17	30 / 20	30	.56	20
	3. Percent employees who drive to work alone	19	10 / 0	15	.79	15
Participation 8	1. Man-hours per month spent by employees in community activity	4,632	50%	+		5,095
	a.) on bank time	585	40	380	1.54	643
	b.) non-bank time	4,047	30	+	↑	4,451
	2. Percent employees donating to United Way	83	20	+	↑	85
	3. Percent employees voting Nov. '74	75	10 / 0			

164

		1974 Performance Level	Net Percentage Performance Differential '73-'74 (2)	1974 Objectives (3)	1974 Social Performance Index (4)	1975 Objectives (5)
Environment 9 (1)	1. Percent office paper which is recycled	18	5% +		▲	18.5
	2. Energy consumed by bank		4			
	a.) steam	44,727,500		44,355,075	.99	44,727,500
	b.) electric (in kilowatt hours 1-1-74 to 12-31-74)	13,095,560	74 3	−15%	.91	13,095,560
	3. Loan commitments to firms dealing in anti-pollution equipment	$8,382,000	2			
	4. Community involvement commitment in man-hours per month	153	1			168
	5. Foundation contribution	$5,000	73 0	$6,037	.83	$5,000
Culture 10	1. Level of commercial line commitments to cultural institutions	$4,000,000	25% 20			$4,000,000
	2. Community involvement — man-hours/month	333	15 10			370
	3. Foundation contribution	$115,200	74 73 5 0	$113,514	.99	$135,200
Human Relations	1. Number minority business loan applicants	56	100%		▲	
	2. Percent approved installment loan applications		80			
	a.) women	82				83
	b.) men	83	60			83
	3. Level of minority business purchases	$46,530	74 40	$45,440	1.01	$49,000
	4. Community involvement — man-hours/month	803	20	+	▲	883
	5. Foundation contribution	$20,500	73 0	$18,250	1.12	$23,500
Community Investment (6)	1. Commitment to lend money to businesses		50%			
	a.) Minneapolis	$284,936,000				$284,936,000
	b.) Suburbs and St. Paul	$296,127,000	40			$296,127,000
	2. Commitments to lend money to civic institutions at other than market terms		30			
	a.) number	8	20			
	b.) amount	$8,700,000	10			$8,700,000
	3. Dollar volume of commercial mortgage loans originated in		73 0			
	a.) Minneapolis	$1,143,000	10			
	b.) Suburbs and St. Paul	$3,902,000	74 20			
	4. Dollar volume commercial construction and land development loans		30			
	a.) Minneapolis	$ 4,685,000	40	+	▼	
	b.) Suburbs and St. Paul	$26,905,000	50	+	▼	
	5. Estimated dollar value of personal loans outstanding/total personal savings deposits	$239,602,000/ $233,568,000		+	▲	
	6. Total Foundation Contribution	$421,000		$420,000	1.0	$445,000
Consumer Protection and Services	1. New consumer services offered	8				8
	2. Diversity of perspective — percent of Board members without a primary background as a business executive	8		+	▼	
	3. Student loans originated in 1974	a.) 1,192				a.) 1,192
	a.) number b.) dollar volume	b.) $1,877,000				b.) $1,877,000

(1) Numbered categories listed in order of community priority as determined from 1972 First Minneapolis community Social-Environmental Audit.

(2) Net Percentage Performance Differential computed by: (a) determining the percentage difference in 1974 against 1973 for each indicator, (b) adding the percentage increases or decreases, and (c) dividing the result by the number of indicators used in the category to determine the net change. Only indicators appearing in both the 1973 and 1974 audit are considered.

(3) Many 1974 objectives were specified only as increase (+) or decrease (−) because the 1974 corporate planning process was not time coordinated with the audit process.

(4) Where a numerical 1974 objective was specified for an indicator, the 1974 achievement was measured against that objective. 1.00 or more indicates the objective was met or exceeded. Less than 1.00 indicates the extent to which the objective was not met. If the 1974 objective indicated an increase (+), the 1974 performance is reflected by an ▲ if the objective was met or by an ▼ if it was not.

(5) Objectives are set as a part of the 1975 corporate management plan.

(6) Entitled Community Commitment in 1973.

Bauer, Raymond A. and Dan H. Fenn, Jr. *The Corporate Social Audit*. New York: Russell Sage Foundation, 1972.

Bauer, Raymond A. and Dan H. Fenn, Jr. "What Is a Corporate Social Audit?" *Harvard Business Review*, January-February 1973.

Corson, John J. and George A. Steiner. *Measuring Business's Social Performance: The Corporate Social Audit*. New York: Committee for Economic Development, 1974.

Dierkes, Mainoff and Raymond A. Bauer, eds., *Corporate Social Accounting*. New York: Praeger, 1973.

Goldston, Eli. *The Quantification of Concern: Some Aspects of Social Accounting*. Pittsburgh: Carnegie-Mellon University, 1971.

Humble, John. *Social Responsibility Audit: A Management Tool for Survival*. London: Foundation for Business Responsibilities, 1973.

Seidler, Lee J. and Lynn L. Seidler. *Social Accounting: Theory, Issues, and Cases*. Los Angeles: Melville Publishing Company, 1975.

DAVID H. BLAKE is Associate Professor of Business Administration and of Political Science, Graduate School of Business, University of Pittsburgh. He is coauthor, with R. S. Walters, of *The Politics of Global Economic Relations*, and is a contributor to journals of business and political science. He has served as a consultant to several corporations, and to the Organization of American States and the Fund for Multinational Management Education. Dr. Blake holds a Ph.D. from Rutgers University.

WILLIAM C. FREDERICK is Professor of Business Administration, Graduate School of Business, University of Pittsburgh. He has served as Dean of the School of Business Administration, University of Kansas City, and of the Graduate School of Business, University of Pittsburgh. Dr. Frederick has been a consultant to the Ford Foundation, the Agnelli Foundation of Turin, Italy, and to several U.S. corporations. He is coauthor, with C. J. Haberstroh, of *Management Education in Spain*, a bilingual text, and has contributed articles to various scholarly journals. Dr. Frederick earned his Ph.D. at the University of Texas.

MILDRED S. MYERS is Librarian and Lecturer in Business Administration at the University of Pittsburgh Graduate School of Business. She is coauthor, with Jay E. Daily, of two cataloguing texts for library assistants, and has written articles for library and business journals. Previously she was Librarian at the Pittsburgh branch of the Federal Reserve Bank of Cleveland. Ms. Myers holds an M.L.S. and an Advanced Certificate in Library and Information Sciences from the University of Pittsburgh.

RELATED TITLES
Published by
Praeger Special Studies

THE MULTINATIONAL CORPORATION AND SOCIAL POLICY:
Special Reference to General Motors in South Africa

> edited by
> Richard A. Jackson

CONSUMER INPUT FOR MARKETING DECISIONS:
A Study of Corporate Departments for Consumer Affairs

> Claes Fornell

ORGANIZATIONS OF THE FUTURE: Interaction with
the External Environment

> edited by
> Harold Leavitt
> Lawrence Pinfield
> Eugene Webb

THE SMALL FIRM OWNER-MANAGER: Entrepreneurial
Behavior and Management Practice

> John Deeks

CITIZENS' GROUPS AND BROADCASTING

> Donald L. Guimary

INDUSTRIAL LOCATION DECISIONS: Detroit Compared
with Atlanta and Chicago

> Lewis Mandell

THE EXODUS OF CORPORATE HEADQUARTERS FROM
NEW YORK CITY

> Wolfgang Quante

DATE DUE

Emphasis '82			
GAYLORD			PRINTED IN U.S.A.